Sing For Me a Quiet and Clean Land

Ingi G. Bjornson

Other books by Ingi G. Bjornson:
Sane Trapper Cooped Up in Remote Cabin With Crazed Wife *(2003)*
Bears and Fine Coffee (2004)
Trapper's Wife Claims to Have Found the Missing Link (2005)
How Many Times Will the Raven Call? (2006)
The Trickling Waters Spoke of a Great Upheaval (2007)
The World Stopped For a Moment (2008)

Sing For Me a Quiet and Clean Land
© 2009 by Ingi G. Bjornson

Illustration by Cindy F. Bjornson, except for the illustration or
chapter 4, which is done by Ingi.
Published by Neso Lake Adventures
Printed and bound in Canada by Houghton Boston

Cover photo: Ingi and Cindy's trapline cabin in Northern
Manitoba

ISBN 978-0-9734608-6-5

I heard the voice of my good friend Bob, and my other good friend Bob, and from Jon, and from John, all having one thing in common: they all knew how to listen well. And they all helped to steer me along in life more than they might know...

One day upon the still waters of Neso Lake amidst the wings of dawn, I heard an oral memo from a man called Remo, "Be careful what you see."

When spruce roots meet birchbark, it's harmony. When a fiddle bow glides over a D and an A string simultaneously, it's harmony. It's also a cup of coffee with a road weary ghost seeker who wanders in off the highway; it's a reunion of old friends.

When Ingi Bjornson asks questions, he asks them from a place of genuine harmony with his Creator and with the land.

Thank you, my friend, for teaching me to be still and to listen for the grace notes.

Ekosi

John Leclair

Sing For Me a Quiet and Clean Land

Ingi Bjornson is affectionately known to some of his friends as "Ingi of the North"... but his stories transcend the restrictions of geography.

He and his family truly 'walk the walk' of good global environmental citizenship, living off/on the land as gently as is possible for humans in the north.

His stories are compassionate and insightful, and encompass an element of spirituality that springs from his ability to slow down and connect with the wonders of Mother Nature.

—Greg East

Contents

Foreword

Then let it be a secret, if that is what it must be. Let the 'conscience of the times' dull our mind and spirit without our knowing it. Let the Indian peoples be seen as drunkards and losers and sub-human and a drain to the non-Indian economy. Then let us, the non-Indians, tell our coarse racial slurs and jokes, let us feel the might and power of standing over the fallen Indian, the broken Indian; then let us revel in the shallow empty victory of which we know not.

Oota nitayan Kichi Manitou Kiwapamihin nikiskeetheeteen—Here I am Great Spirit, You see me I know. May it be that we Your children might seek a little bridge of understanding. May it be that the down-trodden of this nation might continue to grow in strength of spirit; may their cultures and languages and the drum beat pulsate enough that the youth would begin to hear and that roots of hope would grow. And as the down-trodden peoples begin to rise, may it be that the non-Indians would listen to the values which the Indians can, and always could, teach us. May it be, for the multitudes of times that we the non-Indian people have poked our self-righteous finger at the strewn garbage along the roads of a Reservation, mocking the Indians as being collective polluters of this world, that You could help us look back in time and see into the patterns of our own doing that herded the surviving Indians onto the Reservations, hoping they would accept their 'place' in life and eventually assimilate, and that the 'Indian problem' would go away. May it be that You would help us to see through the eyes of a different culture.

If the non-Indian could see through the eyes of the Indian, perhaps we might catch a glimpse of a different form of garbage: Mountaintops blasted away for coal, pristine waters dammed up for more power—flooding ancient homes and lands and bones—vast stretches of land torn apart for oil, various chemicals pumped into the streams so that the fish can no longer live there, and smog so thick that sometimes we cannot see the horizon. May it be that You could help each of us see our own hypocrisy. And may it be that we might walk with You in spirit and in truth.

For those who are the page, and for those who turned the page and began to know the story… For whom has sang the song of a just cause?

Sing For Me a Quiet and Clean Land

It Started

It started, but I could not put my finger on the exact day as to when it started that old had become young.

It was only yesterday that old was old, and I was positively sure of it. I would have bet my life savings on it at the time, though my life savings as a five-year-old were not enormous. As a young child even a 16-year-old was much older and much bigger, a 30-year-old was almost half way through this world, a 50-year-old was very old, and an 80-year-old was as ancient as an emaciated weather-beaten turkey vulture. Yet something happened in life, something so subtle that I could not put a finger on it as to when it all started.

And so I began to ask some very old 50-year-old people who were no longer very old, "When did old age become young?" Most could recognize this phenomenon, but they all had a similar response, they could not put a finger on the exact day when it all began.

I remember turning 16, working full time with my father and uncle in the northern bush. And it seems like only a couple of yesterdays ago that I was suddenly 20 years old. By the age of 20 it seemed like I had almost assuredly passed into the adult-larvae stage. I could use similar nods and body gestures, drink coffee, and talk about politics and weather with even 50 year-old mortals who no longer seemed as old as I thought a 50-year-old ought to be when I was only five. Yet I had paid little attention to this phenomenon, or more likely I was not aware of it at the time.

And now, as I pen these words with the passing of 46 winters, 50 is no longer old anymore, and I would be willing to bet my life savings on it. My body feels good and strong, grateful to breathe in the sweet fragrance of the land. Yet sometimes I catch a glimpse of my face reflected on the surface of the calm water, and I kinda wonder whose face it is that I look upon. It must be the distortion of the water, yet when I see my reflection from a clean mirror in the bathroom I see and confirm that it is my own face that I look into. It seems reasonable to my little mind that it is my reflection: the beginnings of a balding head, longer nose- and ear-hairs, a few less teeth, and wrinkles from kissing the seasons, but something had changed that I could not put my finger on as to the day when it actually began.

There was something about an emaciated weather-beaten turkey vulture (80-year-old final larvae stage) that radiated much more to me than I could see as a five-year-old. It is strange, a seemingly confusing paradox. Yet it was real enough to me that I would bet my life savings on it, which in worldly terms is much more than I had as a five-year-old child. But even my idea of life savings has changed.

By certain world standards I have some money, yet what is having all the money in the world? Will it extend my life another 100 years? True, for several extra thousands of dollars I could have lace or silk fabric or golden handles to adorn my coffin, or pay a higher fee for a cremation by a much more qualified expert: 'Happy Bill's Crematorium! We Guarantee A Complete Burn And Your Very Own Ashes! Get The Very Best Ashes That You Worked So Hard For In Life And Deserve!' And yet, is not ash merely ash? Will not the lace and silk both break down in time? And the golden handles—is that for the worms and ants and mold to admire, or just for someone to later dig up and steal? What then is this game that we dabbled in?

A friend stopped by my camp one day and asked, "So, what's new?"

It was not a new question that was asked of me or to the masses of humanity for thousands of years, yet the same old question had me trying to answer in a satisfactory way. "Well, it's new but it's not really new. You see, as you know, the south wind came visiting yesterday and it pushed the temperatures up above freezing for the first time in four and a half months, and so I snowshoed a couple miles down my secret trail to find a spot in some tall spruce trees that I could lie amid with the spring sun sensuously kissing my face, and I laid there to listen to the first clumps of snow come tumbling down from the trees. They were new sounds, and yet, the more I thought about it they were not new sounds at all, for the sounds of the snow falling off the trees in the springtime have been echoing for many thousands of years."

As I recall, my friend answered back, "Oh."

Perhaps old and young mortals are kinda like the snow that fell from the trees when the sun climbed higher to share more of its strength, each of them causing me to wonder what really is old and what really is new.

It seems strange to me that a 50-year-old person now looks young. How can this be? Has not a 50-year-old always been a 50-year-old? What is this, merely a magician's trick, or the work of an illusionist? Sure, I can kinda appreciate the genetic piecework of our finite bodies, the living cells that can no longer hide so easily the illusions of soft skin and firm flesh, or the vibrancy and passion of youth, but it all happened in a breath, merely the blink of an eye. It really did, and I would bet my life savings on it! We simply could not conceive of this when we were only five years old; there has not been nor will there be any five-year-old who could. Something happened, something so subtle that sought to elude us all.

We sometimes believe the illusion that our lives would be full and complete when we reach the stage of high school, or college, or marriage, or raising children, or a career, or retirement. And yet, to those of us who have breathed the breath of life, all of us, perhaps this chasing and striving was merely an illusion. And if it was merely an illusion, who then was the illusionist? Who is this illusionist that seeks to distract us mortals from the profoundly simple and meaningful things of life? Why does it take so long for some of us to recognize it, that all we really had and have in life is the moment, this very moment? It seems to make less and less sense to me to think that our lives will be full and complete when we reach a certain stage, for the sun rises and the sun sets irrespective of who or what we think we are. Oh, to breathe and have tasted life!

The sun continues to rise and set, as it has done for a long, long time. At 46 years of age the walking and paddling have become easier for me than when I was 20, for the days and the seasons and the land, the handywork of my Creator, have taught me to be more aware of the moment, the only moment that we ever have in our lives. Yet I still find it strange, though not nearly so, that an 80-year-old mortal no longer looks so old anymore, and a 30-year-old mortal looks like a child that has just left home.

Something has changed, something so subtle. I look again, I peer into the eyes of the 80-year-old; it seems odd, as if the whole person is still there, even the twinkle of youth all bundled up into the adult-larvae stage. I saw it, there, like a flash in the dark! Had my senses fooled and deceived me all those years? Have we dwelt more on the temporal rather than the eternal? Have we tried to contain and measure and corner off the realm of time which merely laughed in our faces for doing so? Who are You, Time, that knows no measure? It seems strange, though deep down I knew it was true, that 80 years of adult-larvae and 5 years of child-larvae could be the same to the One who cradles time.

And I saw that the great illusionist was, in the end, no match for the One who cradles time. I could not put my finger on the exact day when it started, yet I safely knew that I could bet my life savings on it; old had become young…

Log Cabins

*Log cabins are
A
Realignment
Of the
Forest*

*From vertical
To
Horizontal*

*The beauty
And
Strength of
The trees
Is
Still There* .

*The mortal builder
Just
Arranged them
Differently*

Jon Donald 06/08

Not Really a Secret

It was not my intent to bore the reader with yet another moose story. Perhaps, then, it was merely an attempt to relive what I thought I lived. Sometimes it bewilders me, how strong the pull is to be on the land when the moose call. And it was not just the call of the moose that I sought, but rather the autumn season and all of the intricate changes and movements of all the creatures that live upon the land.

I was out scouting for some moose sign and movements around September 10th, as they start to become more restless at this time of year, moving about to invisible and mysterious forces, a genetic pull, a driving call of moose foreplay. Walking the short trail back to the lake, there in front of me was a group of eleven otters! Years ago I had seen eleven in one group, eight at another time, but more often the groups consist of four to six otters. And I wondered about this large group: will two families of otters sometimes swim and play together?

It was a week later, on my first night of calling for moose, when an adult lynx walked onto the trail only fifty yards from me, wagging its short, stubby tail. It proceeded to sit and stare at me, quizzical and curious as cats often are. After a couple minutes of staring at each other, I cocked my head to one side, softly meowed, and then walked toward it five paces. I gently repeated this maneuver until I was a mere fifteen yards from the lynx, when it shifted nervously, its comfort zone clearly infringed upon. I meowed once more, slowly advanced four more steps and stopped. From twelve yards away the lynx quickly stood up and walked into the bush. As I slowly walked back to where I had been originally standing, I turned to see the lynx come back onto the trail to sit and stare at me again. In the waning light, I said good night and headed back to camp.

The next evening I called for moose from the same spot and several spruce grouse wandered towards me. A large male with a piece of decorative red on its head flew up on a branch within ten yards of me. I recognized and initiated the seasonal pattern the grouse usually perform during the springtime, but, for whatever reason, also mimic in the fall. I made ten or twelve rapid, small foot shuffles, moving a total of two yards, stopped, and made quick in-and-out breaths through pursed lips while lifting my elbows up and down to the timing of my breaths. The male grouse immediately followed suit, making rapid foot movements, stopped, and making quick in-and-out breaths coinciding with its wings raised and lowered. We repeated these movements for quite some time, the spruce grouse and I, for a half hour or more. It would fly to the ground for its part of the performance, fly back to another branch, and then to the ground again, all within seven to twelve yards of me. In between I would let out some cow moose calls, as I was supposedly moose hunting, after all. I really do not know what was more bewildering to the spruce grouse, to see this man-like being act like a chicken, or to see this grotesquely large chicken let out a moose call. What I do know for sure is that there are many things to discover about the land when the moose call.

Each time I have flown to various areas to listen for moose, my heart was always drawn to the land of my trapline. And so this is the place, for whatever reason, I will go to listen for moose. My big half-breed friend, John, would fly out to join me in six days. In the meantime, my dog Trixie and I would spend six days alone.

Trixie and I were airborne on a frosty morning. She seems to actually enjoy the flights, becoming especially alert when I fly just a couple hundred feet above the trees. The eighty-mile trip to my trapline camp saw us catching up to a slowly receding low pressure. From 1500 feet above ground at the start of our flight, the clouds gradually forced us lower and lower, until we had only 300 feet of ceiling. This was not so bad in and of itself, except that the visibility was now even further reduced by drizzle. We had only 25 miles left to fly when the wall of cloud made my decision for me; I turned 180 degrees and landed on a lake two miles behind us. We taxied to a hospitable shoreline and tied up to wait out the passing weather. Upon stepping ashore, there in front of me was a fresh moose-rub, a clump of alders that was broken and thrashed by the antlers of a bull moose. And I knew the land was alive. And I knew the moose, with all of their fellow creatures, had reason to carry on.

The clouds began to break and lift some three hours later, so we fired up the 160 h.p. engine in the little Murphy Rebel floatplane I had built years ago, and were soon airborne. The skies were filled with snow geese, so extra vigilance was required, although it was quite natural for both the geese and the floatplane pilot to try to avoid each other in flight. As we neared Tulabi Lake the clouds forced us down low again, but by now it mattered little since the familiar river that drained the lake was beneath us, and there is great comfort in familiar territory. Following the gentle curves of the river, we soon reached the lake, landed into a light northeast wind, and taxied to shore.

After unloading the 400 pounds of gear (most of which was for Cindy's and my two-month trapline venture later on), I happened to glance the shorelines, and there, at the south end of the lake about one and a half miles away, was a dark spot at the edge of the willows. A moose! I could not rightly remember the laws about flying and spotting moose and how much time one was supposed to wait after spotting a moose from the air, but it is not my style to hunt this way and never has been. I need to smell and hear and breathe the land. The rut of the moose brings change to its psyche. Usually one of the shyest members of the deer family, during the rut moose can turn into one of the boldest, to perpetuate its species at all costs. Many times the roar of the 160 h.p. engine will chase away moose, but sometimes the roar and the racket will bring one boldly to the shore.

I flipped over the *Super Dam Hopper*, a homemade aluminum boat I had thrown together a couple years ago, which rests beside the original *Dam Hopper*. There are only two of these *Dam Hoppers* in all of North America, quite possibly in the world, and they make their home on my trapline. This 15' x 4.5' flat-bottomed boat was soon in the water with a 15 h.p. engine to push it along. I made my way to the south end, slowly trolling towards the moose that boldly stood sideways showing off a set of antlers belonging to a 2.5 year old. And there, coming into the water some 40 yards distant was a cow and two calves. The calves were also legal game to harvest.

From here on in, I shall try to arrange words with an attempt, feeble as it is, to describe moose as my limited senses have seen them to be, through reading, questions and experience. It is my attempt to arrange these words like a gauntlet, in such a way that certain readers might call me a B.S.er. But arranged in such a way that a few of you readers will feel a sense of recognition through your own intimate experiences, experiences that might leave hints of patterns, that you would know what it is I have seen.

A colourful man by the name of Jim Russell once asked me if I'd ever heard moose call in the summer. To which I answered, "Not since July 12th at 6:30 a.m." I remembered the exact date and time because it had occurred about two and a half hours after I learned that my mother had passed on. And that cow moose and I had called out to each other no less than twenty times while I sat in my kayak 50 yards from it. That particular encounter was a profound one for me.

Jim had a way of talking that held my attention, and his words left patterns that told me he knew the bush in an intimate way. After discussing the calls of moose and such, he asked me another question, "Do you know why people rarely or never hear the moose call in summer, nor hear certain calls of the moose during the autumn rut?" I sat quiet for a minute, and finally said, "Tell me, Jim."

"Because many hunters blast away from a couple hundred yards, so they have little chance to hear certain calls."

It was a sad truth that he spoke, that we blast indiscriminately with high-powered rifles, resulting in a higher incidence of wounded animals. The pressures are great to come home the mighty hunter, with less respect for the wounded creature rather than the dead one to boast of our prowess.

Perhaps, then, it was my motive to share some of these old secrets, secrets that for whatever reason we sometimes hoard, secrets that many of the Indians have known long before the coming of the white man. Perhaps it was my motive to share these secrets (which are not really secrets in that they are known by some), so that not only might we better know the wonders of the land and the creatures that dwell within, but that we might respect the animal we hunt by giving it a better chance for a quicker and cleaner death. I too would be a liar if I said that I had never wounded an animal.

The man is a meat hunter. When he watched a few commercial hunting videos, he was fascinated by some of the footage of moose—the calling, the scraping, the morning fog, the recognition of patterns of body language. Yet, after the hunt, the footage tends to focus on the antlers, the size of them. Where is the footage of how the animal is quartered, how the meat is hauled in and hung up? Is the skin left on or taken off while it hangs, and how long is it hung? Has this majestic animal been reduced to merely the size of antlers it carries? What does this say of the mighty hunter who blasts away from 300 yards with a high-powered rifle at a moose with a large rack—to fill the freezer with meat or to boast of a large rack?

As the man trolled towards the 2.5-year-old bull at the south end of the lake, it started grunting at him "Era-aw! Era-aw!" as it slowly followed the cow and two calves to a willowy point. At about 80 yards from the man, the cow and calves trotted into the water and swam towards the opposite shore. The bull started to follow, but then stopped abruptly to face the man, standing broadside only 50 yards away. It grunted once more and then chased after the cow. The man had committed the unpardonable sin for a meat hunter: he had passed up the shot, but his hunt had only just begun and he had 12 days to come.

This is one of the secrets the man wanted to tell you, though it is not really a secret. It is known by some bow hunters and their guides, it is known by some photographers, and it is known by some meat hunters who call the bull in close for the challenge and intimacy of it all: there is little reason to shoot from afar during the autumn rut. Many aspects of life dabble in the games of hierarchy, from politics to religions to jobs and to hunting. Yet what does it matter to the moose whether its hunter uses a bow, a spear, black powder gun or a high-powered rifle? If the man, a meat hunter, must boast of anything from the hunt, then let it be of a good clean kill.

The previous year, after he had harvested a moose, the man had called in two large bulls, one swimming across the river within 100 yards of him to do battle with the other that also came within 100 yards of the man's call. Each bull appeared to have an antler spread of about 54 inches, fair sized indeed for this part of Canada. The man had called from the shore and now climbed back into his kayak, his preferred mode of travel during the moose hunt, to watch and to join the battle. He played the role of an intermediate bull, with a pair of imitation antlers on his head as he paddled closer to the confrontation. He let out a couple of insecure grunts, and twice during this interchange the biggest moose snorted at him with seeming disgust, "Raa-aw!" as if the man would dare to intrude. It was quite a sight to see these large creature battling and locking antlers, hearing the breaking willows echoing in the waning light of day. Perhaps the man and the bull would meet again someday?

Several years ago, both the man's wife and words from Gandhi had impressed upon him that it is a good thing to keep one's hands busy. When Cindy first said this to him, he reached out to grab her, to which she retorted, "That's not what I meant!" So the man kinda thought it a noble quest to keep occupied during the rut of the autumn moose by trying to study and learn some of the social skills of moose and the land. For whatever reason, the passion has not yet waned over the course of many years, so the man continues to call out and listen to the voices of the land during the whole of the autumn rut.

Here is another secret that is not really a secret at all in that it is known by some: it seemed to the man in his limited experience that the bigger moose seem to relish showing off their size, and they love the call of battle.

Trixie stayed at the camp each evening while the man paddled in his kayak to one of his favorite listening places to call for moose. He would be gone for about four hours each evening, paddling back the two miles up river and one mile along the lakeshore just before dark, where the little log cabin stood vigil. And it is a comforting thing to be greeted by a loyal dog in the dark of night.

On their second day in camp, the man and his dog motored down the river, portaging over a set of rapids where he kept another little boat, and from there they made their way to his little outcamp standing alongside the river, to spend the day clearing some of his trapline trails. A bear had broken into this 'Rainbow Camp' and demolished the interior the year before, though there really was not a whole lot of work to cleaning up an 8' x 10' cabin. After discovering the bear damage last winter, the man had flown in some pieces of metal sheeting, painted gray for some camouflage effect, and screwed these to the cabin exterior in the spring to make it more bear proof. The metal was doing its job just fine; there were several scratches from the claws of the bears, but no bear would easily break in anymore.

There is a sense of delight within the autumn winds that waltz the land, as all creatures great and small, the trees and the shrubs, prepare for the coming of winter. The signs of rutting moose were all about the land. The man and the dog had spotted a cow and calf in the morning, and on the way back they saw that at that same spot a great bull had thrashed a clump of willows.

The third night the man paddled out with his kayak. He started doing some cow calls again, long drawn out higher-pitched tones of "Er-rr-aa-aa-aa-aw! Er-rr-aa-aa-aa-aw!" Around 7:00 p.m. he heard the first grunt, a deep bass that could only belong to the lungs of a great bull, for it is given to moose to have their vibrations of calls according to their size. "Eraa-ch!" It called out infrequently from the same place, and by the pattern of its calls the man knew that it was probably with a hot cow and would not come out to his own cow call. The man was ready to do some bull calls, but night was coming on.

As he paddled back up the river in the growing dark, the full moon rose eerily and beautifully over the horizon to illuminate his way. *Whence come the time of beauty*, he wondered, *and would it be taken notice of?* As the shadows contrasted more sharply and the great horned owl began to call, he knew that night was at hand. He knew that he would be paddling close by the area where the great bull had been calling, and just as he was about to let out a playful grunt, there came from right beside him a snap, and then another, as a cow walked away from the edge of the river. The cow had heard the soft dip of the man's paddle, for moose have ears that hear well and a great sense of smell. And suddenly, (though it was not really suddenly, for it only seemed so to the man because of the short distance) from about 50 yards in the bush came a grunt: "Era-ch!" The man imitated the great bull in like fashion: "Era-ch!" But this time, for whatever reason, perhaps the regular dip of the paddle had thrown a confusion of vibrations, the bull and cow slowly walked away. But just up ahead, a curious calf came to the river's edge only 30 yards away, standing broadside with its ruddy stature strangely illuminated by the night-sun, the moon. And they stared at each other for a moment, the man and the calf, and then the calf turned to walk into the shadowy trees.

Here is another secret, though it is not really a secret in that it is known by some: moose come to the call. It might take five minutes or it might take two or three days, that is for the moose to decide, and the man knows that the moose is much more patient than he is. The man has learned over the years that bulls will stay with a cow for sometimes two or three days, but it will eventually come to check out the cow calls that the man calls out. And that is why the man is content to call out from the same place for many days in a row.

As the man paddles back to camp, he wonders what it is that so enchanted his spirit when he first traveled this little river. Yet, after the passing of many years, there is sometimes the tendency to lose appreciation of it—as with many things in life. Surely the little river has not changed so much, the beavers, otters, mink, and muskrat still travel and live upon it. The ducks and geese nest beside it, the fish swim freely within its flowing depths, the sun and moon and stars radiate their crisp reflections upon its surface. How then, the man sometimes wonders, can this magical enchantment so lose its original luster to him—to anyone? And as he slowly paddles, he realizes, in part, that he sees only as a dimwitted mortal, that he needs his Creator to show him how to be thankful. It is like the illusion of many wrinkles on an old man or woman, the wrinkles he saw on others when he was only 5 years old seemed to look like ancient Egyptian mummies. And now, at 47 years of age, those same wrinkles on older people look so much younger—merely children with dreams and hopes. And yet nothing has changed about the physical wrinkles, nothing at all, only our perception had changed. Because of this, the man began to discover, in part, the joys of the subtle changes of life, the subtle changes of the land.

The more the man pondered the subtle changes of the land, the more he began to realize that he was being watched. At first a growing paranoia began to grip him. It seemed that earlier in life it had been a comfort to be ignorant of the superior senses of smell and hearing that certain animals have compared to humans. Bears, wolves and moose, to name but a few, knew of the man's passing far more often than he knew of theirs. His smells, his sounds—most of the time the man had no idea that he was being watched. But as the years added on, he began to see that his Creator had given certain far-superior senses to the animals than the man possessed, each according to their kind. And he began to realize that his Creator had given certain superior senses to mankind that the animals did not have. For a while the more the man realized how much better the bears and wolves could smell and hear, the greater was his sense of paranoia. And yet, nothing had changed in all of those years, nothing at all, only the man's awareness had changed. For the most part, curious wolves come in close and often howl, perhaps killing and eating a few dogs from time to time, but attacks on people are extremely rare. The bears check out various camps, drawn to the irre sistible smells, mauling and fatalities happening each year, but these are also quite rare. For the most part, bears and wolves avoid direct confrontation with mankind. So nothing had changed, the body language and patterns were still similar, only the man's perception had changed, with a growing awareness of the subtleties of life.

Even as many of the wild animals could sense the man far before he could sense them, he knew that his Creator could sense the wild animals far before they could see the face of their Creator. At first a growing paranoia gripped the man with the knowing that his Creator could see the fibers and motives of all that he was. Each dip of the paddle tended to expose how dim-witted he was to the subtle beauty about him, yet, bit by bit, the magical enchantment of the land began to take on a richer meaning, like the companionable comfort of a good, long marriage. His paranoia began to recede as he began to recognize within himself, in part, his strengths and limitations and flaws, even as he began to recognize the Grace of his Creator. The creatures of the land had merely shown the man, with their superior senses that the man did not have, that his Creator could read his innermost thoughts. And so he saw that it was a good thing to respect the land and all of the creatures that dwell within.

Trixie sat waiting on the edge of the dock for the man,

and she greeted him with a soft wooing call. She is a very loyal dog and stays when the man tells her to stay. The man thought that the dog would give him much comfort should he have to gut and quarter a moose by himself in the dark somewhere, because Trixie would alert him to the presence of bears. Though by this time of year the bears are generally fattened up from blueberries and more intent on their den sites.

It was only the year before that a young bull moose had come into the man's camp after he had called. It was dark and Trixie had initially barked only a few times, but that young bull had come in boldly. A huge bull some years ago had charged Trixie, and she has been nervous around moose ever since. So she kept her respectful, quiet distance, sitting about 50 yards from this now-motionless young bull, even as the man stood only 40 yards from it. After fifteen minutes or so of this quiet confrontation, the bull had slowly walked off. And so the man began to realize that a dog was not necessarily a hindrance during the moose hunt, and he realized that a dog like Trixie, through the recognition of patterns of body-language, could actually be a help to the moose hunt.

That night the man slept outside with Trixie, spellbound by the full moon and two great horned owls that called all night long, geese that flew overhead, and a bull moose that occasionally grunted far to the east of him. It was a hard frost that night. When morning came, the man made a hot cup of coffee and walked to the height of the hill behind camp to call and listen for moose.

It was a quiet morning. He could hear the creek to the east of him spilling over a beaver dam a mile away, and he could hear the roar of the falls five miles to the southwest, but no moose calls reached his ears. He headed back to camp to make some breakfast. Shortly after he finished eating, he noticed the hint of a tiny breeze upon the water. As he looked about, he saw signs of an avalanche of leaves about to fall. He walked over to a group of aspen trees and stood beneath them, his arms outstretched, looking upwards. The leaves were very close to letting go of their summer's grip, and coupled with a heavy coating of frost and the start of a breeze before the sun rose, the man knew that the leaves were about to fall like a heavy, wet snow. The man thought to himself that perhaps it was an honourable calling to watch the storm of leaves begin to fall. As he gazed upwards, he saw how one leaf would fall and bounce on another, setting that one to fall as well, and then those two leaves would knock other leaves off on their chaotic and spiraling float to the ground. As the frosty leaves floated down all about him, landing on his face, shoulders and outstretched arms, and as the stragglers of geese flew over-head to loudly proclaim the autumn season, tears came to the eyes of the man. He wondered where these tears came from, but noted they had been coming more frequently. Perhaps it was that as the man became more aware of the beating of the land's heart, it pointed more and more to the face of his Creator. And the man knew he was not alone.

The next couple of days were windy, so it was hard for the man to hear the calls of the moose. Then, the day before his friend John was scheduled to join him, he flew Trixie home and then flew right back with another load of winter gear. He thought that his companion would be a man instead of a dog for the next week. That evening the winds had calmed, and the man heard the grunt of a large bull just before dark. And as he paddled back to camp, he heard the grunt of another large bull far to the north. He thought that the next morning might bring promise.

Here is another secret, though it is not really a secret in that it is known by some: sometimes the land may seem quiet of moose, and all of a sudden there are three cows, a couple of calves, two fair sized bulls, a medium sized bull and a small bull in the vicinity of each other, all within calling distance. For whatever reason, the moose are sometimes attracted to the area of where the action appears to be, each keeping the distance of their own comfort zones—the receptiveness of the cows and the size and aggression of the bulls.

The next day he awoke early and began calling just before daylight. Within minutes he heard the grunt of a bull to the northwest, so he paddled out to a likely looking spot along the lakeshore and called out a few cow calls again. The great bull gave only a couple grunts, and then became quiet. It seemed to the man that this bull was with a hot cow and would not come out to the man's cow call. So the man tried another tactic—he would play the aggressive bull.

He walked north about one mile along his trapline trail to a rocky height overlooking a small lake, close to where he thought he had last heard the great bull. He was about to call out a grunt, when he heard the big bull start. "Eraa-ch!" Its call echoed in the morning frost from about 400 yards west of the man. The man immediately imitated the call with a deep bass, "Eraa-ch!" And then he took hold of a long dry tree that was lying on the ground and pulled until it broke with a resounding *snap!* that echoed about the frosty hills. Herein is another secret that is not really a secret in that it is known by some: sometimes the big moose like nothing better than to answer the call of a large rival bull. The bull immediately grunted "Eraa-ch! Eraa-ch!" and used its antlers to thrash and break the top of a small tree. The man knew by its body language that it would not hesitate to come to the call of battle. For each grunt the great bull called out, the man imitated it call for call. When it stopped twice more to thrash its antlers against some brush, the man mimicked the sound with just as much or more vehemence.

The man knew by the vibrations of its grunt and the hollow resonations of the paddles of its antlers that it was an exceptionally large moose for this region, ready to challenge any rival. The rocky height where the man called from was only 30 yards east of his trapline trail, separated by a grassy meadow with a tiny creek in the middle that drained the excess waters of the little lake. The great bull stopped once more at about 50 yards, thrashing a small spruce tree with its antlers again, the man doing the same. The vibrations of its call from so close came with greater clarity: "Kk-Eraa-ch!" And again the man answered the same: "Kk-Eraa-ch!" He could not yet see the moose that did not hesitate in the least to join the call of battle, but then, like a ghostly prehistoric creature, it came boldly onto the edge of the meadow, slowly swinging its broad antlers from side to side, confident in its size.

The man, feeling very small and humbled because even a pack of wolves would dare not attack a bull such as this during the intensity of the autumn rut, shot from only 30 yards. The bull shifted slightly, walked a few steps closer and stood its ground. From about 26 yards the man shot twice more, all three bullets tearing through the front sections of lung. Perhaps because the man is not such a good shot is why he tends to harvest moose from 20 to 40 yards. The bull collapsed where it stood. Today the man could boast of a good clean kill.

As the bull fell, the man heard the drone of a floatplane landing by his camp. By the time he walked back to camp the plane had departed, after dropping off his friend. It was good to have company for the next week, and it was even better to have such good company as John. After a fresh cup of coffee, they set about to take care of the moose. The man had a small, three-wheeled ATV that they used to bring the moose to camp. The man would have cut the moose into eight pieces if he had had to handle it by himself, so great was the size of it, but with John along they were able to lift each quarter onto the back of the ATV. The trail was a good trail, and in the span of three hours the whole moose was back at camp. They used a winch-like apparatus to lift each quarter to hang from the strong pole made for this purpose, and then secured each piece with a rope tied around the lower legs cut off just below the knee joint.

The quarters were now hanging on a stout pole in the shade of some spruce trees. It is important to hang the meat in the shade in case the temperature rises too high.

The great bull was the largest the man had ever handled, weighing very close to 1500 pounds. The width of the antlers measured just shy of 55 inches, with very large paddles and some stubby knobs that seemed to indicate the antlers were beginning to decline in size. Antlers are an amazing piece of bone-like structure that grow each year and then fall off during the winter, increasing in size from year to year until the animal reaches its prime, when they begin to recede as it has been given to all creatures to eventually wither and die.

The man hasn't yet had a tough moose to feed on, out of all the moose he has harvested over the years. Here is a secret that is not really a secret in that it is known by some: hang the moose for 7 to 14 days at cool temperatures, the length of time depending on the temperature and the size of the moose. In the food industry this is called controlled rot. The man prefers to hang the meat with the skin left on, as circumstances allow, as the skin with its long coarse hair can act as an insulator and stabilizer in the early autumn temperatures of minus 5 to plus 10 degrees Celsius, helping to keep the meat from freezing at night and helping to keep it cool during the day.

John played his fiddle every day. It was a treat to hear those melodies along the waters of Tulabi Lake, and it was a treat to learn some of the half-breed (Métis) history.

Traveling together in the *Super Dam Hopper*, John came with the man that evening to call for moose, since the man was somewhat more familiar with the river and surrounding land. Just before dark they heard a bull grunt to the north, but it was time to head back to camp. The man knows that each individual has their own way of doing things and needs the freedom to do so. The only compromise he asked John was that, if they traveled together in the boat, there would be no long shots taken, but that they would try to bring the moose and themselves close—20 to 40 yards—because there is no need for far shots during the autumn rut. And there is a pleasure of discovery in trying to learn some of the body language of these great-hoofed creatures that travel the land. John readily agreed to this condition.

Along the river on the way home, they caught a glimpse of a moose dashing into the trees. The man turned the motor off and slowly paddled to where they had last glimpsed the moose. He called out a soft grunt: "Eraa-ch." The snapping twigs gave away the presence of more than one moose. Within two minutes of the man's grunt, the cow called out a soft grunt from only 30 yards away, and then a long, drawn out, soft nasal "O-uh-oo-o-ah. Mwar-oo-oo-oo-aw" that rose and fell in intensity; the call of an estrous cow. To the north of her some 40 yards from within the dark forest came the soft grunt of a bull. The man mimicked the bull. It grunted again and started walking away, its antlers brushing against the willows and branches of the spruce trees that could not hide the resonation of well-developed paddles.

The man and his friend headed back to camp beneath a starry sky. The moon would not show itself tonight until close to 9 o'clock, but the river and lake could be traveled comfortably in the dark of night with the familiarity of home.

The next morning found the man and his friend going for a boat ride to the falls, a seven-mile journey that involved jumping several beaver dams along the way, but the mighty *Super Dam Hopper* was engineered to do just that. They saw no moose amongst the winding course of brilliantly coloured tamarack trees on the way up, most of the birch and poplar trees having already lost their leaves. As they headed back to camp, rounding a bend just before the lake, a cow and bull walked out to the edge of the river about 150 yards ahead. The man immediately cut the throttle to idle, because this is the way he wants to hunt, because there is the joy of discovery in trying to learn the body language of the moose up close. He whispered to his friend what John already knew: the large bull was in full rut and confidently displaying the size of its body and antlers. The man grunted every so often as they worked their way closer and closer. He whispered to his friend that this bull would not run off even while they were up close. The cow turned to walk into the bush while the bull stood its ground, opening its lips slightly each time it called out a grunt. At 25 yards John shot it through the lungs. He shot twice more as the bull slowly turned to walk into the bush. It walked a tight circle, still grunting, and then collapsed. If the man and his friend could boast of anything today, they would boast of a good, clean kill. John searched for some diamond-willow fungus in lieu of sweetgrass, to make a smudge, a part of his culture. He did not find any until the following day, and it is a pleasant and sweet smell.

The moose was gutted and quartered and hauled back to camp to hang on another stout pole. It was another large moose for the region, probably weighing about 1300 pounds. Its antlers had a spread of 52.5 inches, with medium sized paddles.

It is a good feeling to have the winter's meat hanging on stout poles in the autumn landscape. And it is a good thing, the man thought, to have the freedom to ask questions of his half-breed friend, to try to catch glimpses of another culture. To begin to learn such things as the harvesting of the roots of the spruce, splitting and boiling them in leaves and stems to dye them various colours, to be used as a kind of heavy-duty thread. To hear his friend speak the Cree language, and begin to see, in part, that each language holds a piece of the puzzle of humanity.

Before the man and his friend returned to their homes, they had to greatly reduce the weight of the individual quarters so as to ease the work of loading and unloading the moose quarters into the plane and truck necessary to transport the

Sing For Me a Quiet and Clean Land

meat. The moose had to be skinned, and much of the tougher meat trimmed off and placed into large containers, to later be ground into hamburger meat. The rib bones would be all trimmed out, and the tenderloins and backstraps would be carefully filleted out. Later at home, the man and his wife would spend a day cutting and wrapping the year's supply of meat, filling the freezer with satisfaction. It is a pleasant thing to handle and cut the meat of the moose as the whiskey jacks flutter overhead.

The hunt now done, the man filled his remaining evenings by paddling his kayak to his favorite listening place down the river, because he thought it an honourable quest to listen to the voices of the land. One evening, as he made his way there, he paddled within 40 yards of a cow, and within 50 yards of another cow which had walked into the river and swam in the middle of it for 150 yards before heading to the shore again.

As he called for moose, he heard a large pack of timber wolves begin to howl. They were howling from the site of the moose that John had killed, right beside the river, and the man would have to paddle past in the dark when he made his way back to camp. He learned later that John was fishing within 500 yards of the howling pack, and it was a vibration that showed that the heartbeat of the land was alive and well. The man has heard wolves call numerous times every year, and he knows how easy it is for he himself to imitate a wolf call into the night sky and to hear the wolves often answer the call if they are within hearing range of the man. It seems as if the wolves rarely pass up an opportunity to answer a haunting call that echoes about the land. The man also knows from experience that wolves often howl from a recent kill site of animals such as moose. He thought that maybe he would paddle home before dark, since he might have a level of fear when paddling by a large pack of wolves along a narrow, shallow river in a little kayak. But then he wondered about his level of fear, and what to be fearful of? He feared his Creator more than a large pack of wolves; it only made sense that his Creator was greater than a pack of wolves. So he talked to his Creator and asked that he might not be burdened by unnecessary fear, but that he might have a healthy fear of a dark night as he paddled by the gut pile of the moose and many wolves.

The man waited till it was close to dark, and then started paddling back. Far to the north another bull grunted. After two miles of paddling he was within 400 yards of the wolf pack that at this time was not seen nor heard, but the man knew they were there. He paddled slowly in the center of the river, with a knowing that the wolves could hear each regular dip of the paddle, and when he was within 100 yards of the site the words came out quite naturally from the man as he spoke to the wolves, "It is only I, O great hunters of the night. I do not see you nor hear you, but I know you are there. See how the Creator has given you such stealth. I am no match for you. The gut pile is yours, I am merely passing through." When the man finished speaking and dipped his paddle a few more times, he glimpsed a shadowy form move quickly away from the edge of the river only 40 yards ahead. He wondered why he spoke out into the night air to the wolf pack, but it gave him great comfort to do so, and put him much at ease.

Back at camp, John asked the man if he too had heard the wolves. They had not called out for the last hour or so. John then cupped his hands and howled into the still night sky. He was immediately answered by the wolves, calling from where the man had just paddled by. And the man could see that his friend's soul was made well, even as his own was, stirred by the haunting and powerful vibrations of the land and all of its creatures both great and small.

Here is another secret that is not really a secret in that it is known by some: there do be moose about the land, and a host of other creatures, and it is no secret to hear them. Only be still and listen, and you will hear the song of a quiet and clean land that breathes well.

Sing For Me a Quiet and Clean Land

My Shadow

My shadow is able to tell me much, but for the longest time I never really listened to it very well. And it only makes some kinda sense that one could only know as much as one listened.

I have caught a glimpse of my shadow speaking. Well, at least similar mouth movements that I made, with a few distortions depending on the angle and strength of various lighting such as sunlight, moonlight, northern lights, and oil lamps. I suppose that I had merely gotten used to my shadow that was with me all the time, to the point that it was just a tag-along friend that I never even introduced to anyone. I never thought my shadow could teach me anything, or at least little of anything, because I tended to believe that I was the one in control of each and every movement. After all, my shadow could not raise its arm until I first raised mine, and it could not lift its leg until I first lifted mine. I suppose it was this delusion, in part, that fooled me into this arrogant thought pattern.

A moonlit walk on snowshoes along my secret trail gives me much meaning and purpose. Most of my walks are in the daylight, but it made some kinda sense that my shadow might want to also walk in the moonlight, I suppose because of the spiritual wonderment of the clean land lit by magically fluorescent colours. Perhaps the daytime had fooled me into thinking that I did not need my daytime shadow, even though it boldly walked along with me. Perhaps when it was night-time, when I more needed to know that I was not alone because of a greater level of fear of the dark, is why I tended to become more aware and grateful for my shadow and communicated with it more. And it only makes sense.

One night a friend came along with me on my moon-lit walk, both of us anticipating the eclipse of the full moon. We walked in the bush about one mile and made a fire to absorb some warm comforting flames, some coded words of meaning, and the spectacle of the full lunar eclipse. Really, though, I could not fathom all of the hype on radio and television about this eclipse, all of this hype for just a mere shadow. For is that not all an eclipse is—a shadow? Why should the earth's shadow, that was caused by the earth blocking the sun's light upon the moon, create anything more profound than my own nighttime shadow caused by the sun reflecting off of the moon and creating a shadow between myself and little parts of the earth as I moved about? For were they not both merely shadows? After all, had we not snowshoed in the dark to experience the beauty and wonder of a full moon, not a moon that we could barely see?

But as the moon slowly lost its luminance and turned dull shades of beautiful reds and yellows, I realized that shadows could remind us mortals of good and just causes, and the precarious balance of our physical lives. It was almost as if the moon had been turned off for a while (which of course it was), and the sense of stability as I knew it to be was no longer there. I became desperately lonely for my shadow that was always with me on moonlit nights but had now abandoned me. Of course, my shadow had not really abandoned me; it was still there faint enough, though I could not see it with my human eyes. And I suppose it was that faint realm that caused me to wonder a little bit more about my shadow, that when darkness had descended I needed my shadow the most, and it only made sense. And it dawned on me that my shadow could speak and tell me things that I did not know; such as if the moon were to block the light of the sun from reaching our planet for an extended time, there would be grave repercussions. With that I became more grateful for my companionable shadow of the daytime that silently showed that the life-giving force of the sun was with me.

I saw that my shadow could tell me if it was a clear, hazy, broken or cloudy day, and it could tell me if the moon was a quarter full, half full, or obscured by thick or thin clouds. When I had been watching the spinning of the skies around the North Star, as it is perceived by us in the northern hemisphere, and took notice of something so simple as that roughly every 15 degree swing of the Big Dipper's handle relative to the North Star equalled roughly one hour, I realized that my shadow could impart to me much knowledge. This knowledge of being able to tell the time of night merely by the alignment of the stars is, of course, almost as old as the hills and the first peoples to travel them. It is just that in these perceived modern times of wealthy nations it is simpler just to look at a wristwatch instead of the stars' alignment. Besides, when great wealth has come together with cities full of multitudes of enlightened people and towering skyscrapers with lights that are never turned off so that one cannot even see the stars of the night, a wristwatch is also practical. Though don't forget that the timekeeping of a wristwatch was greatly helped along by a mere shadow: a sundial. The thrust of a watch is merely to tell us what time of day it is, but people have had this technology for many thousands of years, merely by shadows.

As long as there have been people there has always been shadows accompanying them; some people more aware of them than others. As much as my shadow was fading as the shadow of the earth obscured the moon this night, keeping pace, my shadow was showing me of things to come. And, even as the night grew very dark for a while, my shadow slowly, minutely, began to show itself to tell me that the sun's light of the moon would indeed come back with even more brilliance, because, in part, of the greater knowing and appreciation for my shadow.

I realized that my shadow could tell me exactly how tall I am, and at what latitude I might be standing on this little world, and what time, day and month of the year it was. (It would not tell me what year it was, because the year is merely a baseline which various mortals have chosen to base a sense of time and history on, the various calendars in this world seeming to be based on something perceived as significant in history.) This knowledge of height, latitude, time, day and month is, of course, as old as the hills and the peoples who long ago began to travel them, and a tape measure, watch and Global Positioning System would speed the process up much faster than my shadow could. But Cindy had told me to keep my hands busy, so I kinda thought that I could keep better occupied without looking at a watch or tape measure or G.P.S. Our shadows have been freely given to us, to ignore or to embrace. Either way they would reflect a shadow of things to come.

The sun, for me, was much more consistent and stable than the moon with regard to its brightness, and required much fewer calculations than that of the moon. Also, it is the sun that gives light to the moon, all of which is why I trusted the sun to help me along in life. The sun offers light and life to the world for everyone; you see, to find out this knowledge was a simple matter of listening to my shadow. All I had to do now was pick a spot where my shadow was better seen, any spot on this world that was not blocked from the sun's light. If a building or mountain was in the way, just move or climb to the spot where the sun was better seen; a crowd of people sometimes distorted the many shadows, so to better see one's own shadow may require a solitary place for a while. Snow and rainstorms would come and go, smoke and haze would try to obscure, long winter nights of the arctic, and fog so thick and for so long that some people might begin to lose hope of ever seeing the sun again, but if you looked close enough a general trend would begin to emerge and the patterns of things to come would make a little bit of sense.

I chose a spot along my secret trail that wound its way through the boreal forest. The calculations for beginning to know who I am, how tall I am, where I was, or if I was known were becoming for me as real as my shadow on a clear sunny day. You see, I knew via the North Star that I was in the northern hemisphere, and I knew through the knowledge of others that the North Star is at 90 degrees above the horizon when viewed from the North Pole, and at 0 degrees on the horizon when viewed from the equator (which could help one to calculate the latitude on a clear night). I knew by the song of the land whether it was spring or autumn. I knew that by choosing one spot and standing there without moving in the daytime, my shadow alone would tell me the highest spot of the sun by my noting the shortest cast of my shadow, which would be high noon. And by making daily calculations as the days allowed (some days were cloudy and stormy, and some days were bright with hope), factoring in my height relative to sea level, calculating my shortest shadow from summer's high noon to my shortest shadow of winter's high noon, when the sun rose and set from winter to summer—I could pinpoint the exact latitude of where I stood on this world. And with these calculations known it would be merely a few calculations of triangulation of my shadow that the sun made known to me relative to where I stood that could figure out my exact height. By knowing these calculations my shadow could relay to me who I am, and that I am known.

If I had used a simple wristwatch, tape measure and G.P.S. it would have greatly speeded up the whole process, but that's just the point. With greater speed life may become merely a blur, and those tools could not calculate for me what I truly needed to know. And so I began to know that a reference point in life is needed to show us where we are and who we might be. That is why, of course, it made sense to listen to my shadow.

Why Trapping is Important

It was only a vision of a little log cabin with a covered porch, a row of split firewood just outside the front door, a blanket of snow on the roof with a few icicles along the edge, a splitting ax embedded in a stump, and lazy curls of smoke that slowly rose to begin the journey of wherever the wind carried it. It was a picture that I drew for many years since I was a child, the thoughts having come from various books of the North that my eyes could not turn away from; stories of dog teams, wolves, moose, marten, wolverine, lynx, the migrating geese, and all of the creatures that dwell within the land. A land where the snows and ice came to stay for a big part of the year, where the pine and the spruce danced to the autumn winds, as if dancing in celebration to the changes of the land. I told my young friends that when I grew up I wanted to become a trapper. Some asked me why I wanted to become a cruel animal killer, and it was a question that I had no answer for. But the vision of the little log cabin would not leave me alone. It was there during my schoolwork, it was there when I lay down at night, it was there when my friends talked about large motors and girls and sports, and it is with me still.

Forty-five winters have now graced my trails, and I have still not grown up, nor gotten into sports or fancy motors, but I do have myself a fine wife for 21 years now. Why, I believe that I acquired the best gal that a trapper could ever ask for; she flies out to our remote trapline every single year with me, she skins fur, fillets fish, packages moose meat, cooks, sweeps, mops, bakes, edits, and whacks me over the head with a frozen broom from time to time as I require it, which in her opinion is often. What then do I do... uh, other stuff?

I've run registered trap lines for 28 years in a row now, having missed only one year. The year that I did not trap was when my wife and I were in the Yukon trying to pursue a trapline up there. My wife became homesick for the boreal forest in northern Manitoba, and, to speed up the story, we headed back to our familiar turf and acquired a remote fly-out trapline some 80 miles southwest of Thompson. My family and I have flown out to this remote area every single year now since 1991, from early October to roughly mid-December, with no restocking or sight of another soul for the whole dura-tion.

Perhaps my hardest decision as a father was the deci-sion to fly our two sons out with us every year since they were one and three years old. Communication with the mobile phone service was, at best, working about 50% of the time. I could accept it if sickness came to me and I died on the trapline just from the pursuit of some silly childhood dream, but I did not want my young sons or wife to suffer because of my childhood dream that would not leave me alone.

Sing For Me a Quiet and Clean Land

The years have passed by, because it is the nature of the years to freely pass by, for time cannot be corralled or seized, but time does allow us to ask questions and to wonder what it is and why it is that we pursue certain things in life. I have lived and breathed the air of a quiet land, a land free of roads and concrete, a land that has tried to teach me to listen and to be still, and I can no longer separate my Creator from the steps of my snowshoes. Our two sons can always go to visit the cities of humankind, but it is a much rarer opportunity to have known the trails of the trapline. They will leave home soon, and we will miss them. They will probably chase life and girls for a while, but perhaps the memories of the trapline will come back to visit them at times when life appears to be complicated and busy, when the business of life adds on to the hours, and the hours to days, and the days to years. Perhaps the memories of the trapline—the stillness of the land, the howl of the wolves, the grunt of the moose, the first frosts on the sphagnum moss that no longer melts, the haunting melody of the first ice that echoes the song of the ancient ice-dance, the fresh fish or grouse that sustained us, the long shadows of the trees that told of short winter days, reading by the light of the oil lamp, snuggled up in a mighty log cabin that contains the warmth of the woodstove—perhaps these memories will come back to them at appropriate times in life when they most need the comfort of the simplicity of life, and it only makes some kinda sense?

Whence come the autumn winds that waltz the land? When the geese once again begin their flight south, my heart leaps with youthful excitement even as it did when I was but a child. For I know that soon the moose will be calling, there are wild blueberries and cranberries to harvest, the red squirrels are chatting away as they gather the cones of spruce trees, the beavers are gathering their winter feed together and building their dams, the leaves have lit up the countryside with their fluorescent golds and yellows and reds, the tamarack trees' needles have changed. It seems as if the whole of the land is preparing for the long winter ahead, and it only makes some kinda sense.

Shortly after the peak of the rutting moose, we will need to be flown into our trapline camp on Tulabi Lake to beat the freeze-up. Like clockwork we are flown in every year around October 10th. The land has gripped my soul more than I know; it is not that the land needs me, rather it is that I need the land. The lynx does not need me, nor do the marten, for they have been on the land a long, long time. The trapline trails have helped me to see my need of the land about me, for when my heart is heavy from the trials and sadness of life, I will paddle or snowshoe to a quiet place to chat with my Creator. When the lynx has chased down and eaten the snowshoe hare, or the forest fires have burnt through the old growth trees, or the summer rains have flooded the land, what is that to me, for these are things that are needed from time to time. You see, the land is still here; the morning sun continues to rise in the east, the creeks and rivers continue to flow their way back to the seas from which they came. When I hear the call of the raven I know that a new day has begun, and when I hear the call of the great horned owl I know the time of night is at hand. From the front porch of the trapline cabin my eyes can see the start of one day passing into the next, and then yet another day has passed. Soon the years will have slipped by, so it only makes sense to give thanks for today, for today is the day that is always with us.

It seems a paradox to me, to harvest the pelts of the marten or the lynx or the wolverine, to put a price tag on the skin of an animal that is surely worth more to the animal than it is to me. Yet my walking along the trapline trails has helped me to better see that life cannot be had for free, for life can only be had by consuming life. The vegetation needs the land, even as the snowshoe hare needs the vegetation, even as the lynx needs the snowshoe hare. We need the molecular structure of water to sustain the vegetation, the hares, the lynx, and the humans, for without it we would die. If life is life, then it allows me a reasonable question: "What species is more deserving of life: a plant, a mosquito, a rat, or a timber wolf?" So who in society will dictate to us which species is more important than another? The interconnectedness of life is an intriguing, little known, and delicate balance, but what we do know for sure is that life carries on in some way. The songbirds come visiting the boreal forest in summer to feed on such things as mosquitoes. What I know for sure is that a dead songbird sings no song, but a fed songbird sings a sweet song. And so in turn the mosquitoes will help to feed the hawk, and the mosquitoes will help to feed the marten that helps itself to a songbird's eggs.

The trapline trails have helped me to see that there is a price tag to everything in life, from mosquitoes to eggs to water to oil to humans, and this has all helped me to better understand the question I was asked by my childhood friends of so long ago: "Why do you want to be a cruel animal killer?" Indeed, in some ways it does seem a visibly cruel way to make a living, that of harvesting the animals, but the land of my Creator has molded me more than I know, and it has been more than a privilege to walk the trapline trails. And so I must learn to respect the land, I must harvest without harvesting too much, I must be diligent to harvest the animals as humanely and respectfully as possible. To respect life while knowing one must take life in order to live.

Why trapping is important to me is because it helps me to recognize the smell of the beaver as I paddle along the edge of the river, it helps me to recognize the bark of a fox on a winter night, it helps me to recognize and to imitate the snorting of the river otter as it often swims to within 15 yards of my canoe, it helps me to recognize the autumn winds that waltz the land, it has helped me to look deeper within myself; and a cry rings out from my soul.

Good travels…
Ingi G. Bjornson

This essay for International Trapper *magazine won first place in Fall 2006.*

Global Warming

The world—our little planet—has maintained a constant and spinning stability for a long, long time; long enough to hold the life of ancient fish and dinosaurs. The ice has always been somewhat restless, advancing and receding, the ocean waters rising and falling, but there has been, at times, enough constant to provide stability for different forms of life to flourish for many years. There was a time when our world was so hot that no life (as we know it to be) could survive its gaseous, nuclear, molten state—seems to me that the burning of fuels might have contributed to that molten state, and we could not even blame Shell or Syncrude for that fiery mess. But over time our world cooled, and for that I am grateful because I never was too fussy about breathing in an air temperature of 2000 degrees or more. It's kinda hard on our lungs.

Lately I heard folks talking about a dangerous man-made global warming, apparently caused by such things as the burning of fossil fuels. And if there is any truth to this at all, why, I highly suggest that we go after those darn oil consumers! And, uh, oh dagnabbit, I just drove 20 miles to town the other day to take my wife out for a cup of coffee. It was not my motive to contribute to the supposed greenhouse gases, I just naively wanted to take my wife out for a cup of coffee and a muffin. I apologize for this, as we could have just as easily made some coffee at our camp instead of burning the fuel required for a 40 mile round trip.

One time a fellow wrote to me how distressed he was after watching a well-known movie that told of the dilemmas facing our world due to global warming, yet in the next sentence he wrote of looking forward to an extended trip he was taking to places in South America. I do not know how much fuel per capita it costs for a mortal to fly in a jet from Canada to South America, or to any other far destination for that matter, but it must burn up more than a few gallons of fuel, many of the large jets using upwards of a thousand gallons per hour. I kinda got to wondering how much fuel per capita we might burn up by going on an ocean cruise? Now, I ain't one to talk, as even my illustrious little business has me flying about 40 hours a year in a little floatplane, burning close to 300 gallons of fuel per season.

It is a paradox that we, humanity, are caught in, for human nature that has been fairly constant will not be uprooted so easily. Bring on more fuel efficient vehicles with greater comfort, clearer music, smoother running, and we will simply travel faster and further, burning just as much or more fuel than the original efficiency might have sought. If there is any truth to this global warming from such things as the burning of fossil fuels, then let us go after those darn oil consumers like myself. Have we no choice but to legislate against our own selfishness over which we have so little control?

We are supposedly the enlightened generation, driving

our children to organized sports and piano lessons almost every day of the week so that we might try yet again to give our children a better chance in life. (Well, I guess this doesn't include the poor peoples of our nation.) Sure, there might be some events that are more local and within a short walking distance, but we have vehicles that travel smoother and faster, and the wealth to do it, so we might as well drive further. Gosh, it really must be a kinda sacrifice some parents do indeed make for their children, because I have heard some of them express how worn out and busy they are from all this driving around almost every day of the week. Cheer up, you are obviously making life better for your children. After all, what merit could there possibly be from staying home and playing games with your children, or having a wiener roast or walking or paddling a canoe or building snow forts or sliding or playing catch with a ball or talking or curling up with popcorn to watch a movie together, things like these which will obviously not give your children a better chance in life. Besides, by driving every day all worn out, you still have a future to look forward to for your children by burning up all of those extra fossil fuels and putting on extra weight at the same time: a warming planet, if there is any truth to this global warming. Gosh, doesn't this seem to be telling me that we have to spend more money to be rushed, disheveled and warm the planet all at the same time?

Why is it that I must play the naïve dummy so often? To play the game of which I am accused of, and yet it takes very little effort—I suspect because deep down that is all I really am. Ah, to know the joy and pleasure of conversing with a wise elder by the campfire, to converse with anyone of any age or any background or any colour who allows the freedom to ask and to be asked questions, to speak well and to listen well. I seek not an expert geneticist or scientist or scholar or priest or trapper when searching for pieces of truth, for my life is too simple and uncluttered to have any time for them, I merely seek all of the above who can communicate with a measure of compassion and humility—a knowing that we are each of us stupid in the greater scheme of things. Through it all my wife is my constant.

Now, if there is any truth to this, uh, global warming, why, perhaps it makes some kinda sense to go after some of the bigger culprits to get the most bang for our buck, although we ought to include almost every citizen that lives and breathes and walks this planet. So I kinda think it only makes sense to look into different political ideals that might encourage or discourage the burning of these fossil fuels. Who or what was it that was responsible, in part, for supposedly helping to offset the delicate balance of our world? Prior to the Industrial Revolution there was a lot less intentional burning of fossil fuels. But the Industrial Revolution, coupled with the protestant work ethic (defined by *Webster's International Encyclopedia* as a set of values that esteems hard work, thrift, duty, efficiency, and self-discipline, identified with Calvinism; that a person's time and talents are gifts from God and that prosperity is a sign of piety and salvation. Apparently the concept of a protestant ethic was formalized by the German sociologist Max Weber in his essay "The Protestant Ethic and the Spirit of Capitalism") helped to ensure that more wealth would be created, making possible a more general prosperity. This caused a growing dependence on fossil fuels as humanity just had to spend our new wealth somewhere and on something. After all, how could we express our sophistication and status by merely going for a walk in the woods or a paddle on a quiet lake? Who would then see our wealth, for what is wealth if there is no one to show it and compare it to?

Now, in all fairness, we cannot just lump the whole of humanity into the context of the protestant work ethic. But we, humanity, seek to sometimes understand life by quartering concepts and ideas and theories and such within the confines of labels and pamphlets and columns and graphs.

In my own little mind I cannot put the primary blame of global warming, if there is such a thing, on just the labeling of a protestant work ethic where prosperity might be a sign of godliness (does this infer that contentment with having little in life and finding immense pleasure in walking through the forest or paddling a canoe upon a quiet lake might send a person straight to the pits of hell?), for human nature has greater common denominators than just a narrow printed label. Unless my eyes have greatly deceived me, I cannot see a whole lot of difference between Canadians and Americans regarding the acquiring and hoarding of material goods—whether they be Protestant, Catholic, Muslim, N.D.P, Liberal, Conservative, Republican or Democrat, plumber, doctor, or a street bum, each tending to individually spend within the boundaries of what they bring in monetarily.

Hang on, you readers who may take offence at this general lumping of humanity and human nature, for I have merely used generalities to seek patterns of codes. I realize that each race and culture has a remnant of selfless people. People who are more community rather than individually minded, those who might seek to do their part to lessen the smog and exhaust in our air, those who have found contentment with a simple walk through the woods or with the song of the paddle. However, to me a label such as capitalism, regardless of political or religious views, seems as good a culprit as any in regard to the increase of the burning of fossil fuels that might help promote a warming of our planet, that is if the burning of fossil fuels does indeed have a great impact on our planet.

Free enterprise: the freer we are as individuals to pursue our individual enterprise, the greater the capacity to create more wealth both individually and collectively. Or uh, our greed is let loose to pursue our individual needs plus a heck of a lot more, and this greed in turn is cushioned somewhat by the measure of existing socialism within the existing pecking order of our capitalistic structure. Unless, of course, I have grossly misunderstood the workings of our politics and human nature.

Now, we should not give a free ride to those bent towards a more leftist/communist lean regarding the burning of fossil fuels, places such as the former Soviet Union or China. These countries have kinda helped to foul our air as well. True enough, countries such as the former Soviet Union and China succeeded in creating large military establishments under the banner of communist rule, but often failed to provide some of the basic needs for their people, including food. (Though the U.S.' and Canada's system of economics has also left a few people on the streets, and residues of colonialism have left us with such things as Indian reservations and black ghettos.) It just goes to show that every political ideal has its own pecking order. Of course, we all have our own pecking orders in things such as the military, unions, construction sites, school administration, schoolyards, churches, and even within our own homes—at least I do. I'm reprimanded by my wife as required, which seems to be often.

Under the banner of a more communist rule, without private property, where a doctor might earn less than a factory worker, communal farms and such, there may not be the same incentive to take care of a building, more room to mistakenly replace a heart for a kidney during surgery, or just do the minimal share of work on a collective farm and stop for coffee breaks an hour or longer. Of course, I've been guilty of hour-long coffee breaks on an almost daily basis.

Now, I should not be too hard on a political ideal other than the one of which I have experienced in Canada. I was just merely trying to establish that we are all of us incentive driven one way or another. If a doctor is paid $200,000 per year there is more incentive to try to make sure that a heart is not replaced by a kidney, as a dead patient can be kinda hard on business. Though Canada itself has thousands of serious complications and deaths each year from the many mistakes of doctors and nurses—to be human is to err. We have more incentive to stay in our well-paid union job, in spite of its own pecking order and challenges, that we might maximize our sizable pension. And we tend to maximize our potential crops and work long hours within the context of private property to maximize our profit. This in itself should not be seen as evil, the basic human need to stay alive, as even the squirrels store up a pile of cones for themselves—of course the difference here being one of need and one of want.

If all of the multi-national oil corporations could make the same money right now on more eco-friendly power sources as they do on oil and all of its invested infrastructure, do you think we would quickly see more things such as cleaner burning vehicles? Of course we would—all things in life are incentive driven in one way or another. Would we dare to flood the lands with mega dams, or pour coal and various nuclear elements into the behemoths that generate power and not seek to get our money back on our investment? Given the choice would the shareholders choose an 8% or a 35% annual return? Which would you choose? Far be it for the electricity corporations and all of their shareholders to strongly and genuinely promote energy efficiency for the sole sake of cleaner lands any more than those who fought to keep the black slave trade alive and well to "protect their investments". And yet, what greater song has risen from this sinister trade than John Newton's "Amazing Grace"?

We with the vested interest will protect our investments at great cost, making a pretence here and there of efficiency as the marketplace allows, taking great pains to promote illusionary eco-friendly entities as the opportunity allows, while the flooded and ravaged lands and tainted waters and fouled air give testimony. Where are these mega-efficient solar panels and air-compressed engines and why are they not yet mass produced? Far be it for the individual citizen to have the sun and the air for free, why, that might upset the balance of wealth and power.

We would dance to the ring of the Profit Bell, mesmerized by its seductive allure. As we hacked and coughed amidst the smog that obscured the sun and shunned the dirty waters of the stream that the fish fled from and looked about the landscape of concrete and steel that made cursed the home of the buffalo and the wolf and the grizzly bear we would chant, "The American Dream is mine!"

Here be a riddle: if the sun and the air are indeed free, walk, paddle, sit by the bubbling brook, breathe in deeply of a quiet and clean land that your spirit might be refreshed, kiss the sun and the elements often enough, as you are able, so that your face might boast a tanned and weathered look, proof of a sensuous affair.

I was merely trying to establish code patterns for myself, relationships between politics and human nature and global warming (if there is any truth to it) to find out who the culprit might be. All nations and all people create a measure of individual and collective wealth within the confines and freedoms of the pecking order of their national politics. Human nature does not differ within any of our various political swings; political swings have merely had to work within the confines of human nature. Those of a strong leftist/socialist view may not have the same incentive to maximize the building and maintenance of the best automobile with the least emissions, due to less individual wealth, although fewer different models are built and the vehicles are generally kept going for many years. A strong right view may have more incentive to maximize the efficiency of building and maintaining the best automobile with the least emissions, but our increased individual wealth generally has us buying much more fuel and traveling further distances, or buying a new model every few years, completely annulling any gains from the fuel efficiency.

Nations with great internal strife, civil war or ruled by tyrants, may subdue its people and keep them from pursuing anything but the most basic requirements of life such as food and shelter. This system of those in a nation only seeking the basics of human needs has always been easy and user friendly for our planet, unless of course the numbers of displaced people are large, which is often the case since the population of the human race is at an all time high and growing. The more uprooted and unsettled a nation is, the more its buildings are burned, its trees are cut down for cooking and for warmth, the animals of the land are hunted down regardless of a national park's border—all driven by the basic need to survive.

What is a terrorist? Whom is it that has terrorized the fish that struggle in tainted waters or the birds of the air that might struggle in fouled air or the animals of the land that have fewer places to lay their head? Do you not hear it? And all of creation sings for a quiet and clean land...

Okay, perhaps we might be able to agree, in part, that human nature is fairly constant and has been for thousands of years. And perhaps we might be able to agree that humanity—of which we are all a part—is a bit of a tangled web. Indeed, everything is a trade-off in life.

All right, lets go get those darn oil consumers, that is, if the burning of fossil fuels such as oil helps to contribute to our supposed global warming. And uh, oh shoot, some time has passed since I started this story and I guess I just took my wife out for another cup of coffee. It was not in my heart to purposely and maliciously contribute to global warming (if there is any truth to it) by burning up 1.5 gallons of gas by traveling in our mini-van that gets 38 mpg and listening to one of Cindy's favorite CDs while the inside air was adjusted to a comfortable temperature, when we could have made coffee at our camp. I just wanted to take her for a romantic drive and a cup of coffee with the extra coins of wealth that could purchase this all.

Do you not begin to see the codes and patterns? Human nature is what it is and will not be uprooted so easily, just as it hasn't been for thousands of years. I call the bluff and call it boldly. We, humanity, will not slow down the burning of fossil fuels which some believe causes global warming, if there is any truth to it, because we would first have to slow down human nature. This is not possible; we can only try to work within the confines of the dreadful and joyful part of being human. Humanity has played the games of the haves and the have-nots since the time of our first neighbour. All we needed was one neighbour to test a piece of our human nature, to test its swing from joyful contentment to wanton covetousness. It is a historically tragic pattern that we often seek to covet rather than to be content. To those poorer nations of our world who might see the material wealth of rich nations through formats such as Internet and television, it is only natural for many to want what they do not have, far beyond the basic needs of food and shelter. The examples of the rich nations of this world will help to encourage the want of the poorer nations for whatever it might be—democracy, giant houses, fast cars, and food, so much food. Cars will be built at a feverish pace within the supply-demand marketplace, complementing the increased burning of fossil fuels. The marketplace of supply-demand itself, which we blindly follow, will be the primary decision maker as to when mass-produced alternative-energy vehicles will become available. The Profit Bell-god must not be offended.

However, there is One other player that will overrule the Profit Bell. When our planet's growing fouled air and tainted waters and ravaged lands and all of its creatures cry out in anguish to the Creator, their cry will not go unnoticed.

We can only try to seek alternatives and to legislate in some form, via the powers of the people, we the government, to help curb the power and danger of our own selves. To help curb the power and danger of the large multi-nationals

(Colonialism or Roman Empire substitutes, a mere manifestation of power) who are merely mortals like ourselves who have acquired a greater level of economic power within the political context of the times. We, humanity, in one way or another are driven by incentives. The development and mass manufacturing of such things as more eco-friendly vehicles will come more easily and much quicker as the supply ratio of oil can no longer keep up with demand. The wealth of the large multi-nationals will not be uprooted so easily, and we as individuals will do our part to support more off-shore drilling and the tearing up of lands and developing places like the tar sands to support our individual and corporate gluttonous habits. (People kinda like myself who take their wife out for a cup of coffee in their mini-van.) And we will support the warming of our planet—that is if there is any truth to it. After all, lest we forget, we are merely giving our children, ourselves and humanity a better chance at life, aren't we? (Okay, humanity in the previous sentence might be kinda stretching things a little, as it is and always has been a select number of mortals holding the wealth.)

I don't really have much more to say about global warming, that is if there is any truth to it, except to write a couple of suggestions. After all, it just ain't right to point fingers at culprits such as myself without giving a couple of constructive suggestions.

Stop purchasing and drinking bottled water in our rich nations, I've never drunk one in my life. Egads, we're paying more for bottled water than for gas, though gas is starting to rank up there as well. The tap water in our communities goes through stringent testing. True, we will always have occasions of human error with a few tainted water issues, but by and large our water is safe. Besides, what guarantee do you have that bottled water is safe to drink? How much fuel and labour is there required to haul and distribute these multiple truck-loads of heavy water? How much toxins are spewed into our air from the making of the plastic bottles? How many empty bottles are tossed along the roadside or into our lakes and streams? Water, one of the essential ingredients needed to sustain life on our planet, and now we haul it across our nation in trucks, and get this—in airplanes—so that we can help to burn off more fossil fuels and have traces of oily leaks from our trucks washed into our streams and lakes by the rain. Egads! Just buy one container, and keep refilling it from the tap of your home or from a northern stream or lake that the animals and birds drink from.

If you have an errand to do or a small package to pick up that is only one mile away, walk. It is true that by walking you may miss out on a favorite song on your CD, the controlled temperature of your heater or air conditioner, and the feeling of a mighty mortal in control of 4000 pounds of steel. But by walking you will begin to feel the elation of your lungs contracting and expanding, hear the songbirds, and lessen your visits to the hospital. What is it to you if your neighbour has a big truck or a big house or a fast boat? Stand apart and have the freedom, the profound freedom, not to be bribed so easily.

And, oh darn, I really want to take my wife out for a cup of coffee again. The desires are so great of seeing other people, trying to maintain social skills, a diversion from the sameness of the household. Even the illusion, the elation of the voyage of discovery as we burn off those fossil fuels that have fooled us into thinking that we might see more and become wiser because we have traveled further and faster. Dang it, why is it that whenever I look for the culprit I see it in the mirror? Perhaps a compressed-air engine is in order… But how will I heat it in winter when it's minus 30 degrees?

The world, like the swing of politics and religions and economics and theories, the swing of opinions which we all at one time or another utter for merely to breathe is to have an opinion, will take care of itself. If we price ourselves out of the marketplace through the strength of unions and high wages and pension plans within a capitalist structure, there is more reason for companies to move overseas and to import from places like China.

If a nation like China continues to maintain a one-child policy for whatever reason, with the parents often siding on keeping a male child, the demographics of a lop-sided ratio of males to females will catch up with itself and cause its own challenges, and it will take care of itself. If a nation was to practice a rigid political form such as Apartheid (Afrikaans for "apartness"), a system separating a ruling minority of white-skinned mortals from a majority of Africans, Asians, and coloured, and the segregated majority was to rise up, there would be an uprooting of a nation, even the oracles of time have known this. Did you not see the story within the concrete walls and metal gates surrounding the home? What possible reason could there be to build a monstrous gate around a family's home except for a greater measure of safety against a greater measure of fear, a greater measure of a minority seeking to protect its haves from the majority of the have-less and have-nots.

There would always be remnants of peacemakers and seekers of understanding from within all colour groups and races and cultures seeking to build a little bridge, but the majority would rarely see or seek to know an understanding. For to better know an understanding is to better see ourselves for what we truly might be—a piece of the monster. The more we talk rather than genuinely listen, the greater the degree of not gaining an understanding, and it only makes sense. We, humanity, tend to reap what we have sown, both as individuals and as a nation. The turmoil, the monster who dwells within all colours of skin, would be let loose to seek its own equilibrium, as if the turmoil could see beyond itself.

The patterns were all about us as we breathed and lived, vivid and pulsing and chaotic patterns each with their own coded heartbeat, and it greatly troubled the man to catch a glimpse of this knowledge, it troubled him to the core. We would walk the trail of which we know not, so that he thought, God help us all.

If there is any truth about increased global warming caused, in part, by the increased burning of fossil fuels, it too will take care of itself. We, humanity, thought that we were in full control of the vehicle in which we drove. Perhaps some of us will catch glimpses that, all along, we never were much in control, blindly driving along into an illusion of which we know not.

And oh…sing for me a quiet and clean land that breathes well.

"O God, if I worship Thee for fear of Hell, burn me in Hell and if I worship thee in hope of Paradise, exclude me from Paradise; but if I worship Thee for Thy own sake, grudge me not thy everlasting beauty."
—Rabi'ah al-'Adawiyah (d. 801) a woman from Basra in Iraq

When I Retire

There ain't much sense in retiring just yet, although in Cindy's opinion I have been retired for many years already. Don't know what she means by that as I put in just as much time as any other mortal—about 24 hours a day. I'm only 47 years old at this writing, so why would I want to retire? It don't make much sense to me.

My days are always busy with something and my calendar is full, each day having a number on it anywhere from 1 to 31. These numbers kinda save me the trouble of having to write something in the little square boxes.

I get kinda confused with the idea of 'moving up the ladder' in this world in order to better our retirement. If I move up on the side of the world that I travel on, it only makes sense to me that someone on the opposite side of the globe must be moving down; or is it me that is then moving down?

Where is this illusionary place called up? And what of the coded words that say 'What goes up must come down'? Do we rise to our perceived success only to be brought down by an old broken body that once again wears diapers? It seems to me, then, that the description of the word up is merely a coded word translated to defy the forces of gravity, and that is why of course I also have the goal of moving up in this world to plan for my retirement.

It seems that we mortals sometimes like to corner time into seconds, minutes, hours, days, months and years—to somehow tame time in a fashion that we could understand and relate to with our finite minds, to somehow stabilize the realm of mystery, the unknown. But time will not be easily persuaded to stand still and be cornered, it just is. We try to somehow measure time, but with all our effort, is it not merely the spinning of our little planet that tells us roughly 24 hours, and its tilt that gives us the seasons, and its travels with the sun that gives us a year? If we lived on a different planet somewhere else, we would then have to find a new relative measure of time to reflect that which we might want to measure.

When I grow up and retire I want to be whatever it is that others might perceive retirement to be. Seems to me, from what I've heard and read, that for some people retiring has something to do with a sense of freedom—to do what one wants to do, to travel where one wants to travel, or not be bound to a schedule. Alas, I don't think I'll ever be able to retire based on those ideals, because sometimes I want to go canoeing but the lake has just frozen over, and sometimes I want to walk with snowshoes across the swamps and ponds but I have to wait until they are frozen over, and I am bound to the non-ending schedule of the calendar. I generally can't call for moose until they go into rut in the autumn, I can't travel the land to harvest fur until freeze-up and snow arrives, I can't hear the ducks and the geese until spring arrives, and I cannot see the full leaves and blueberries and warm waters until summer has been. How can I ever hope to escape the mundane of life, the same sun that rises and sets, the moon that fills and wanes, the same wife and the homemade bread that she makes, day in and day out?

When I retire I would like to have a good wife, a couple of fine children, a good dog and a little log cabin by the edge of a quiet lake with a quaint outhouse to the side. I hope this ain't asking for too much. Perhaps it is?

Sometimes people say they retire, have a party and receive a gold watch, but then I see that they just go back to work again in the same job, perhaps this time on a casual basis. I guess this might be so that they can maximize a full pension, and then make yet more money by going back to work—kinda like double dipping. Don't make much sense to call this retirement; it kinda looks like just a monetary promotion sometimes.

It makes some kinda sense to me to store up a few dollars to help counter the days when we become older and more feeble and unable to handle much physical work. Heck, even the squirrels store up cones and the beavers store up willows, birch and poplar for the coming winter, so planning ahead a little seems sound to me. But I ain't never seen a squirrel or beaver gather stockpiles of feed all year round for several years in a row just for a huge pile to look at. Why, they might be dead before their time seeing as they left out any playing or visiting. Seems to me sometimes that mortals try to stockpile a large pile of money and material possessions, far more than the basic requirements for food and shelter, but I guess it must be kinda neat to have a big pile of money and things to look at. Unless of course one had neglected to play and visit during the accumulation process and then died earlier than they thought they might. Someone else will just inherit that stockpile of money and things when we're gone anyways. And I kinda get confused sometimes because some mortals had described retirement as having the freedom to play and to visit at will.

When I grow up and retire I want the freedom to do what it is that others want to do when they retire. Why, I've heard of people who seem so passionate about something, doing their darndest to get others on board to help uphold these passionate beliefs in whatever it is that they might believe. Yet, when the time comes that they might retire or take on a different job or role, we see these feigned beliefs often fall by the wayside. Perhaps it was committments connected to their work, or school committees or a kids' club that they lose interest in after their child graduates.

I want to see how the shoemaker takes care of his own family's shoes after selling the customers on the kind of shoe they should buy. I want to see how passionately the mechanic might take care of his own family's vehicle after passionately telling the paying customers what needs to be done to their vehicles. I want to see how healthy a nurse or a doctor and their families might be after they preach about eating and living healthy and the dangers of being overweight to paying customers. I want to see how passionate a priest or a pastor might be about the inner knowing of our Creator that is not dead after they might preach for many years to their congregations. I want to see the relationship a psychiatrist might have with their own family after they explain to a paying customer the problem with theirs. I want to see how much gas a politician might personally burn off, how efficiently he or she might live, after preaching about the possible dangers of burning fossil fuels.

You see, sometimes our passions in life are merely linked to the monetary pay we might receive to carry through with whatever it is that we are expected to do, and then when the paycheque stops so might our feigned passions. This kinda confuses me sometimes, and causes me to think of what the difference might be between genuine-passions, and the incentives of bribed-passions of whatever occupation we might dabble in. And so it is kinda intriguing for me to look into what we as individuals might be passionate about in life when there are no monetary or other rewards, no stars to put on our résumés for the sole sake of trying to make a résumé seem more glowing, no goods or services benefits coming our way at all.

I want to be what the welder wants to be when he or she retires, I want to be what the schoolteacher or doctor or nurse or politician or pastor or priest or miner wants to be when they retire; when this perceived sense of freedom might come upon them and they are free to pursue their unbribed genuine-passions of life. I want, I need, a glimpse into my, our, lives that might relay a piece of the code of what it might be to be human and what it might mean to be truly free in life.

I hear that retiring can take a little planning, what with major changes in life sometimes. Working from 9 to 5 for so many years, and then all of a sudden having the choice of not working 9 to 5 anymore if one does not want to; sleeping in past 7:00 a.m. on a weekend if one wants to; kinda like a sense of freedom? Guess I do not have much freedom yet, because I rise out of bed around 6:00 a.m. every morning, on weekdays and weekends. My habit on a winter day is that I rise to put the kettle of water on, light a fire in the woodstove, put on my coat and boots to walk outside and have a leak and look about to see if it is clear or cloudy or calm or windy. When I come back inside Cindy is up and pouring hot water through a filter to make good coffee. I close the damper of the stove that begins to embrace us with welcome heat, and sit in my chair with a couple of books. My wife brings me a steaming cup of coffee and I sip it slowly, sensuously, for a good cup of coffee ought not to be rushed. She takes her coffee to the bedroom where she curls up in bed with a book, and I sit with mine with my dog Trixie curled up beside me. Ah, a precious quiet hour or more of reading, with the only sounds the crackling of the fire and the breathing of Trixie.

There is no reason to be up early, and yet there is, for the sounds and experiences of the conscious early morning cannot be had from the snoring bed. There are just not enough hours in the day to do what has to be done. Well, actually there is and always has been for every mortal dead or alive, even the squirrels and beavers know this. Is it not merely our attitudes and perceptions that cause us to speak and think in certain ways? Or did you think that our Creator was so dull and short-sighted in the way that our world was aligned to spin and to orbit around the sun in the course of a year-plus-6 hours? Will we, as mere mortals, somehow force our revolving planet to spin slower so as to add more hours to a day? And then what, will we still say that there is not enough hours in the day to do what has to be done? Go then, to the barren rocks of Mars that has more hours to its day so that you might complete what it is you thought you might complete if there were more hours to a day, and then learn to yearn for the bountiful planet called Earth that you left behind. Did not ancient words decree "Be still, and know that I am God"?

Where then is this world that we might think is a rat race, and what does this have to do with us as individuals? Who is in control of the moment, the very moment, that we hear our breath that allows us to live and move and have our being? To breathe in is to know I am alive, to breathe out is to know I have lived. Who or what is it that would take away from us the knowledge of the moment? Ever-consuming career advancement, rushing here and there, for what? The chase of a perceived better life that goes far above our basic needs of food and shelter so that we might have a pile of goods and money to look at for when our bodies whither and fall apart from old age? When I retire, I would like the freedom to get out of bed whenever I want to.

It is a strange word sometimes: *inflation*. The logic of an inflated balloon or an inflated ego or an inflated advertisement makes some kinda sense to me, but the inflation of goods and services eludes me sometimes. And yet it is so that we mortals sometimes push for higher wages to keep up with this illusionary inflation. When I retire, I would like to have shelter and food, after all, is that not a universal need for all peoples, for all creatures of the land? Within the animal kingdom, if the animals are fat they live in a season of plenty; if they are thin they live in a season of want. According to this analogy, we have at this time, by and large, enough food and shelter for most of the peoples of rich nations—and still we must pursue ever more beyond our basic needs to prepare for our retirement. And for what? To die with a hoard of goods by our side, old trinkets that are thrown in the garbage because we could not throw them away ourselves, or a pile of money that we think might define our success in life? Yet this word *inflation* eludes me sometimes.

I, too, received a substantial "raise" last year, as in each year prior to the previous one—an indexed wage increase that no union nor government at any level could prevent me from receiving, they were all powerless to effect any change to it. You see, it is merely by breathing that I, we, receive our indexed wage increase, and was it not all an illusion—this engine of greed? I received a raise for picking wild blueberries and cranberries, for harvesting moose, for drinking the water straight from the lakes and creeks, and I will expect another huge wage increase this coming autumn. My indexed wage increase was aided by such things as the growing of bio-fuels, which of course helped to create food shortages in many countries, which of course puts, and always does put, the biggest drain on poor countries, which of course magically raises the price of grains and foods, which of course will increase the death rate and the poverty levels in some of the poor countries for a time, which of course helps to make a mockery of those from rich nations who had boasted about ending world poverty—but at least it helps to ensure more fuel for those of us wealthy enough to drive our cars and trucks.

Someone knew this would happen; who are you and what is your name? Even the man can figure this out with his grade 10 education, that there is only so much agricultural land and only so much water. Who are you that rings the Profit Bell that we might blindly follow its call?

I received a substantial raise this year from the dead trees that I harvest for firewood to heat our little home, because the demand for oil and energy keeps ever growing. And the land that Cindy and I live on is apparently worth a little bit more just because someone else's land is apparently worth more. So here be a riddle: nothing had changed—the moose is still a moose, the wild berries are still wild berries, the tree is still a tree, the fresh water is still fresh water, and the land is still the land. Have we not merely succumbed to an illusion? What has changed, in part, because of our individual and collective greed, is that as our wealth grows so does the tendency for our growing callousness to the subtleness of the sacred. *Forgive us, Creator, for the ever-rising prices we put on the blueberries and cranberries, the water and moose and trees and the land. You know it is our own folly to think we are masters of the land, to think that we can measure the land by a price tag, or to look at the living moose and to arrogantly tell it how much it is worth. What is our worth as mortals today as You look upon us? The Land and all of its creatures, all of its life, has always had one constant price—precious. Help us to know this.* I suppose, then, that it be a good thing to check out our investments and stocks of goods to see that we might have enough food and shelter for our retirement.

Alas, it is my wanton greed and folly if I have asked for too much when I retire, but in my heart I am guilty of still seeking it: A quaint little log cabin hewn from the local woods built near the edge of a quiet lake, smoke rising from its chimney and the smell of fresh bread wafting about. A little outhouse to the side, close to the woodpile so that I could bring in an armful of wood after sitting on the throne. A wife whom

I could not have asked for any better. Two sons who have given me joy and who have made me proud of them especially since they have come from such an imperfect man such as I. A loyal dog who will not back down from any bear, and a Creator who is not dead. But really, the more I think about it, is there much sense for a man to seek that which he already has?

A Quiet and Clean Land

When the volcanoes
Ceased
And the earth
Cooled

When the rain
Stopped
And the sun
Shone

When the ice melted
Then began
A
"Quiet and clean Land"

Jon Donald—2008

Sing For Me a
Quiet and Clean Land

I am understood, fully and completely, known as much as I possibly could be known.

It just came to the man in those words, as crisp as the night air while the moonlight glittered and sparkled upon the snowy surface. It is not so unusual for mortals to desire to be fully understood, to feel within that we are known and always have been known. Nor is it compatible to be both completely known and yet alone; if this be true, then it only makes sense that we are not alone. For what reason is there to be understood—our passions and reasonings and follies—if not to communicate to someone else, something else, something beyond ourselves?

It was not a radio program, book or university classroom that brought this piece of (what the man believed to be) truth to him. He had merely dressed himself with a couple of extra layers, including a heavy sweater and coat, to help keep warm while he sat in the outhouse on the frigid moonlit night. True, the invisible frequency of radio waves were all about him, memories of books lay in his subconscious mind, and there was little doubt that his comfortable seat with wide open door rivaled the view of any university classroom. That is, of course, if a moonlit night that radiated its sparkling presence upon the frozen lake and snow-laden trees while the great horned owl called could compete in some way with a professor trying to describe class 3 or class 7 amortization, shareholder structures or deferred taxes to a group of half-sleepy accounting students.

And yet, it was within this one-person classroom that the man suddenly realized that he was and is fully and completely understood. And the more he began to think about it, the more he realized that there was more than one being within the classroom that he took part in. The land spoke and, bit by bit, the man began to hear its voice. It was like invisible radio waves that are all about yet we cannot learn to discern until we are finally drawn towards the tuning dial. Something had kept us from reaching within ourselves. Perhaps it was health, a fat bank account or the goal of having a fat bank account, the ease of life as we lengthened the girth of our belt, the ease of life that made us yearn for something of more meaningful value. The land always could and did speak, because that is the way our Creator had made it to be.

Some would describe the land as 'wilderness' or 'wildness', or something to be tamed and harnessed by civilized mortals. And yet, even after a substantial portion of the world had been tamed by civilized mortals, it still had not tamed and harnessed the soul within each and every one of those same mortals. Something was still missing. Could it really be that the land had, and always did have, a living voice, a spirit voice that carried the presence of our Creator? Did you not hear the land speak? Sing for me a quiet and clean land.

Even this Jesus, who claimed to be the Son of God, the

Word made flesh, the very Creator, did not go to the towns and cities and the ease of life to be tested. It was recorded that this Jesus went to the 'wilderness', where He fasted and prayed for forty consecutive days to be tested. What is it then, the man wondered, that the land might have that could actually test us? Who or what would keep this Jesus accountable in His hermit-like odyssey—a tree, a rock, a stream; the soft song of a quiet and clean land?

The man saw that the cultivation of lands and killing off of different creatures that our Creator had set in their places was not enough for restless mortals. Some mortals knew that the ever taming of lands might lead to the ever less-ening of our world and the diversity of its creatures, and of our individual spirit within. And some mortals knew that thou-sands of years of tamed lands had proven that, even with all the growing wealth and ease, it was grossly inadequate to the taming of our individual souls within. For even as some want-ed to ever consume and alter and tame, there were those who caught a glimpse of something beyond themselves and were, for whatever reason, persuaded to set apart pieces of land. And so, pieces of lands would be set aside. *National Parks* some called them, and it was the intention that these pieces of wilderness might be set aside from the ravaging commerce of human nature. Some mortals were naïve enough to think that these new parks were now safe for all time, protected by a mere political border, a mere stroke of the pen. Yet even a fool could see by reading into a few pages of history, both old and new, that political borders and their ideals could change almost as fast as the ocean's tide.

It seemed strange to the man that we need laws and enforcement to control the beast of our individual and collec-tive glut and want, for was it not like saying that we as indi-viduals and humanity could not be trusted? If we could not be trusted, it only made sense to the man that therein must dwell the realm of good and evil. The man knew this with a growing awareness, because he knew that the laws were not made just for others, but were made first for himself, and then all of humanity. And if the laws were made first for himself, then it only encouraged him to listen, and to wait, for the song of a quiet and clean land that breathes well.

It was good, the man thought, to set aside pieces of land from the ravages of humanity, from the ravages within us all that we desperately want to believe is not there. Others yes, ourselves no, but it is there, in varying degrees, in all of us. Just by being we consume. Just by being educated we consume more, the man thought, for does not the academic interpretation of education often lead to better and higher paying jobs? And with this extra wealth is there not a tendency to spend more on material goods: bigger homes and cars, jet and ship travel, ATVs and large boats? And when we seek a diversion from chasing commerce, do we then sometimes travel to our Provincial or National Parks and bring these noisy mechanized pieces with us for our quiet getaway, even as our waistlines increase?

Sacred places, spirit places, are words the man had read and heard used to describe National Parks. Yet what mortal would be bold enough to call a National Park, a sizable tract of relatively untouched nature, a sacred place? For could this not spawn thought patterns of 'spirit', within and without, conceivable room for the Creator? Could this not spawn the thought pattern that, deep down, each one of us consists of spirit? Perhaps it is an honourable quest, the man thought, to create National Parks, to leave behind a reminder of some semblance of order and sanity and sacredness to all forms of life. But the man knew, because he always had been fully known and understood within and without, that the spirit pulse of the land could not be contained within the exclusiveness of a political boundary like a National Park. So sang the song of a quiet and clean land that breathes well.

It seemed strange to the man, when he tried to think

Sing For Me a Quiet and Clean Land

about it all, that he was and always had been fully known and understood. For it was only normal for mortals to, deep down, seek to be at least partially understood by one or two close friends, or perhaps by a marriage of sixty years. Or perhaps paying thousands of dollars to some stranger playing the role of a psychiatrist, a complete stranger working for a handsome fee, to try to garner some insights as to who or what we might be. Throughout all of history it was true, and still is today as the sun rises to proclaim a new day, that mortals desperately need to be known, when all along perhaps it was merely the aching desire to fully know that we are not alone? And yet, it was as real to the man as any vision that he might have had, that he was and always had been fully known and understood. It was not that the man understood himself fully as to who or what he might be, when in reality he understood himself so little that he did not even trust himself, it was just that the vision he had of being fully known and understood gave him a profound sense of comfort. It only made some kinda sense then that he had a Friend, and if he had a Friend it could only mean that he was not alone. So sang the song of a quiet and clean land.

It seemed to the man that he began to be more aware of his Creator in his travels of quiet lands by paddle or by foot, especially on his trapline. Even at the time of these words, the nearest road of any sort was still about twenty-five air miles south of his little log cabin. It was sometimes hard to make this understood to other mortals, that here, by his little log cabin, there were no roads, no malls, but only vast areas of rolling hills and lakes and creeks and rivers within the Precambrian Shield.

Ka Kanata Askiy, the Cree words meaning 'The land that is clean'. *Kanata*, the word from which *Canada* came. But, in many places, as many of the Cree elders and others knew, the land was no longer so clean. The buffalo were killed off to make room for the vast hordes of immigrants. The restless pursuit of commerce and the perceived 'better life' involved blasting away mountaintops, flooding huge tracts of lands with mega-dams, clear cutting the forests, dragging indiscriminately the ocean's bottom with huge nets, mass penned and fed cattle, and playing with pesticides and herbicides both on large farms and even on the tiny lawns of individual home owners who might still have the gall to complain of tainted drinking water. Drilling and tearing the ground for oil so that we mortals might travel further and faster and longer with greater comfort—traveling with movies and music and drink and food. All this wealth so that we could no longer hear the soft song of a quiet and clean land that breathes well.

Even within so-called sacred places, National Parks, the battle between encouraging commerce or leaving the land untouched and natural was strong, as evidenced in parks like Banff. Millions visit this park each year, to catch a glimpse of what? A majestic mountain view from a $300-per-night room, a souvenir trinket from one of the various businesses, or to walk a trail that has been trod by so many people that the print of the grizzly can no longer be seen? Yet even with all these growing pressures and distractions, the man knew in his heart that there are those who go to places like Banff to seek and to hear the soft song of a quiet and clean land.

It seemed to the man that, to a greater or lesser degree, we are all of us bribed in life. If a Parks Canada worker, lower on the perceived pyramid, strongly voiced his or her opposition to yet another thirty million dollar expansion that was endorsed or at least okayed by upper management, who thought that perhaps these extra revenues could help make Parks Canada more self-sufficient monetarily, this lower caste worker might be severely reprimanded or fired. But if the man voiced a complaint of disappearing clean lands, how would he be reprimanded? What would they fire him from? Would they take away the beaver dam that he laid beside as he listened to the voices of the trickling waters? Surely at some point within a National Park, a sacred place, there must be an end to the ravages of commerce, or there will simply be no room left to blast and tear and build. All of this spending, all of the hype, millions of people; did you tell them that the mountains and rivers and trees could speak? And if they speak, how could the voices be heard over the masses of people? Deeper into the woods and mountains they had to go, the wolves and the grizzlies and certain mortals, to better hear the soft song of a quiet and clean land.

It seemed to the man that his trapline was a National Park to him, and if some mortals laughed at this, in his heart he knew it is a sacred place. He knows that perhaps he has not greatly erred in trying to treat the land as sacred, something that the Creator had placed here for the life of the birds, fish, animals, and the man. What could he offer the lake after catching a fish for supper, what could he possibly give back that the lake needed from him? To the man the answer came easy: he gave thanks. He gave thanks for the bounty of the land that his Creator had made. He gave thanks for a quiet and clean land.

It seemed strange to the man that on his roughly 120 square mile trapline, there were no roads, no other mortals living there, only the little trails that he and his wife and two sons had cut over the years. The bears, wolves, moose, caribou, lynx, wolverine and fox, to name a few, would follow these trails even as the man had followed portions of natural game trails when making his own trails. His trapline seemed National to him, because within the realm of politics the land belonged to the Crown, the government and citizens of Canada. And it seemed a Park, because of the manifest and natural beauty, untouched by the ravages of commerce. This is why it seemed to the man that his trapline was a National Park—a sacred land, a land set apart to be clean, a land to remind us that we are and always have been known, a land to rejuvenate our spirit that we might soar. *Ka Kanata Askiy*! The land that is clean! Canada, oh Canada!

True, the man brought in about six hunters a year, harvesting five or six bears a season. The man harvested the marten and the beaver and various other creatures, each in their ebb and flow of the intricate web of nature, as the land allowed from year to year. And he harvested one or two moose a year, as well as fish, berries and grouse. The man harvests a fraction of what is killed off just by the non-stop army of vehicles that drive through Banff, a train of traffic so thick that the timber wolf could cross but part way, flattened and bloodied by the moving tons of steel and exhaust. The man's trapline was natural and clean, the embodiment of what some, deep within their hearts, hoped a National Park could be. Yet it seemed very strange to the man that there was not a four-lane paved highway to his little log cabin, why there was not a mad rush of gold-fevered or lonely mortals who desperately needed to know they are and always have been known, rushing to this sacred spot. For the land abounds in gold and gems and diamonds, and the land held the secret code, the very combination that might unlock our soul to let us know that we are and always have been fully known and understood.

The man knew that he was not lying, for he had seen these precious gems every year. When the autumn winds come visiting, the land lights up with fluorescent golds and gems of all colours, and the early frosts sparkle like countless diamonds on the moonlit night. The wolves call freely, the wolverine travels at will, the moose grunts with satisfaction and the geese help to herald the changing seasons, so that the voice of the land is heard. Everything was here, all about him, it seemed to the man: the call of a wild land, a sacred place, untouched as yet by the ravages of commerce, all the requirements for a truly National Park.

On a busy year there might be twelve visitors. Perhaps one day it might rise to twenty, or perhaps drop to six per year. For to most (and the irony was not lost on him) this land with its long cold winters and hot summers full of mosquitoes was merely a harsh wasteland only to be used to ravage the forests and the rocks as commerce dictates.

It was this same wasteland, *Ka Kanata Askiy*, where the man had the vision that he was and always had been fully known and understood, and he knew then that all along he never had been alone. Sing for me the soft song of a quiet and clean land that breathes well…

Sing For Me a Quiet and Clean Land

Bears Habits and Humans

In 2005 I was given the okay to move my black bear hunting allocation from Guthrie Lake to Tulabi Lake. My reason for requesting this change was not to chase an illusionary rainbow that held better fishing or better bear hunting, but only because it made practical sense for me. You see, the vicinity of Tulabi Lake is where I have run trap lines for many years now. I already had a fuel cache, boats, and a fine log cabin there to stay in with a covered porch that works well when I want to sip a hot coffee on a rainy day. Tent camps continue to leave fine and pleasant memories for me, but flying the camps in and out costs money. Whereas hunting from Guthrie Lake had involved setting up a tent camp every spring and a flight of 67 air miles, Tulabi Lake offered a permanent camp to stay in and lay only 25 miles straight north of the community of Snow Lake. Not to mention that a piece of my heart laced with lovely memories resided there. When the opportunity came to take hunters out to my trapline camp, my decision was made in half the blink of an eye.

Feeling pretty sure that this change would be approved, in autumn I built a few tree stands along the edge of the lake and a few more along the edge of the river, to prepare for the following spring bear hunt. I placed them along areas of high ground, close to my established trapline trails that were kinda like interstate highways for the bears to travel on. Many stretches of these trails have shown well-worn bear tracks over the years. It is only natural for creatures like bears to follow a path, something they create themselves; they are creatures of habit as are we. It is no mystery as to where to choose hunting sites. I spaced them apart about every two miles, in areas of higher ground to keep the hunters' feet dry, allow easy access with the boat, and, most importantly, the sites could double as my own personal spots to call moose in the fall time. Indeed, important business decisions must be made by important businessmen sometimes.

Some outfitters might call setting up hunting areas work, but I could not call it work at all, for all I saw was adventure and discovery in one giant playground. Sweating and toiling beneath the sun and rain only make the woodstove and hot coffee back in camp all the more sweet. There are other things in life that I might label as work, but not the out-fitting business.

I have heard it said, and also read, that a fellow ought not to travel alone in the backcountry, for if one gets injured the consequences could be dire. Can a man mock this sound wisdom? No, I will not mock it. But dos and don'ts are not always applicable in every situation. I have spent decades traveling alone along the trapline trails; it is who I am. So who wins in life: the one who dies in a hospital bed surrounded by doctors and nurses, or the one who dies alone on the trapline trail? Where indeed is the most appropriate place to die?

Which mortal is more secure and free: one who must live within three blocks of a hospital, or one who lives amid the natural hinterland where a minor injury could lead to death? In the end, who has exercised the folly of denying our spirit within?

Minor injuries and serious close calls can be good for a mortal, for they remind us of who we are   fragile human beings that are here today and gone tomorrow. These things can help to temper and sober us and remind us to walk in a more safe fashion, such as testing the first ice with the axe before one crosses it, or throwing an old wooden ladder away and building a fresh one every so often. Indeed, more than one mortal has perished in remote areas of the bush from a simple broken leg, bedridden for many weeks until they expired. But I'd best get started on yet another bear hunt.

Hunting bears from a baited site may be defined by some within the hunting hierarchy as being at the lower end of the sporting measuring stick. One can suppose that this may have something to do with the ease of hunting as you sit in your stand, the lack of sweat, or the minimal skill of stalking that is required, basically saying that a 95-year-old grandma would have no problem whatsoever in harvesting a bear at a baited site. Gosh, so much for the fishing industry with its big boats, swivel seats, trolling motors and fish-finders! How about the everyday usage of computers and television instead of listening to the land, shopping at a grocery store instead of snaring rabbits, driving a vehicle to work instead of snow-shoeing, indoor plumbing instead of an outhouse, designer underwear, using elevators, eating in restaurants, or sleeping in late in the morning? I kinda assume that some of these sug-gestions must be awfully low on the hunting hierarchy scale as well, because of the lack of prowess and sweat that is need-ed to get the job done.

I was already on my third trip flying in with my float-plane to check on the bear activity around the hunting sites.

The sites were all being visited by black bears, especially my camp by the lakeshore, which I told the hunters is just one great big bait site come springtime. Indeed, because of harvesting big game and various fur-bearing critters over many years, the camp is full of smells that brings in many curious black bears, especially in the early springtime when they have emerged from their dens after a long winter.

The early stools of springtime give evidence of what the bears eat fresh out of the den, things such as green grasses, remnants of the past autumn's moss berries and bunch berries, and poplar buds, each in their timing as the sun regulates their growth. Stool does not hide its evidence so easily, showing that the bears are quite choosy in what they consume when first coming out of their dens, selecting foods that are easy on their shriveled stomachs. In time they will feast on suckers, a carp-like fish, as these swim in the rocky shallows of the rapids to spawn, a meal free for the taking. The bears leave evidence of this feasting by the packed-down dirt and old grasses full of scattered large fish scales. There is no mistaking the large scales of the suckers.

It is not a scary thing for me to fly out to the trapline camp by myself, put the boat and motor into the lake, and cruise the shorelines and river to check on the bear signs before the hunters come in. There is always a rifle in my hands at this time of year, as it is not unusual to walk up on a bear at the hunting sites or by the rapids full of spawning suckers. But my heart always skips a beat and then pounds at a feverish pace when I am bluff charged by a bear, especially when I'm by myself. Many times the bluff charge signals that there might be some cubs nearby. You see, it is possible to learn some of the bears' body language when one cradles a loaded rifle, for the fear of the unknown may be overwhelming when all one has on hand for self-defense is a four-inch long pocket knife or an old handkerchief.

From what I have read and gathered through conversation, within the black bear family it is not the sow with cubs that causes the majority of injuries or death to Homo sapiens. Though grizzlies, I understand, are a different story. I have read that many of the serious black bear encounters involved two- or three-year-old bears, juveniles perhaps testing out their new grounds of freedom kinda like invincible teenagers with beer in their hands, or older bears who might for whatever reason have a harder time acquiring food. My two, what I believe to be, serious encounters with bears happened to be with older male bears. These fell the way of lead poisoning at 10 and 15 yards. Had I only a dirty handkerchief or a four-inch knife on hand, the outcome may have been substantially different.

Indeed, it is a difficult thing to try to sort out our passionate perceptions, our personal experiences in life. If one has been jogging and has surprised a black bear sow with two small cubs at a 20-yard range, it is only natural for the sow to try to protect her young ones. Yet the same sow with cubs that has been spotted at 50 yards while the same person is walking would have produced a different story. Some of the hunters from the lower 48 have been a little skeptical when I tell them that it is, for the most part, quite safe to walk up to a tree that black bear cubs are in. To prove this point, on several occasions I have indeed walked up and placed my hands on the very same tree that the cubs were in. You see, the cubs feel safe; this their mother had taught them from their first wanderings away from the den. They will lie and sprawl amongst the branches in quite a relaxed fashion, and, because they are in their safe zone, there is no reason to whine and whimper, calls that might bring mama bear to defend or at least come a little closer with a bluff charge. Great beasts of the forest, like bears, do not want to risk personal injury, because injuries can mean pain and future difficulty in acquiring or defending food. This is why bluff charges are so much more common than actual encounters. And so there are beasts and mortals who sometimes call the bluff.

Sometimes in life, for whatever reason, we might break or challenge the rules, one of which might be: Do not feed the bears! Recently, I broke this rule. A sow with three cubs had frequented our camp the previous summer, though by late summer she only had two cubs left, one brown and one black. This sow was very bold and confident around our two barking dogs, and after bluff charging them on several occasions as I stood close by, she began to completely ignore the dogs and nibble on green grasses or tear open a stump to look for insects, leaving her cubs in a tree. Numerous times she wandered our yard with her cubs safe in a tree, sometimes in the spruce tree that was only three yards from our house. Anyhow, this same family showed up the next spring, not long out of hibernation. After a half hour had passed of furious barking from our dogs, huffs and puffs from mama bear, and bluff charges from both parties, mama bear decided to once again ignore the dogs and lie down and nibble on some grasses that had retained a semblance of greenness from last summer. And so I broke a supposed rule for a confident mama bear and her two cubs. I grabbed an apple and slowly walked towards mama bear, talking softly to her and congratulating her for surviving the long cold winter. At about 18 yards I stopped, cut off a piece of apple with my knife, and tossed the piece to her. The reaction was instant: she was drawn towards the scent and gratefully devoured the piece! I cut another and again tossed it towards her, she again gobbled it up and looked towards me. I continued talking softly to her, "Hello, mama bear. I'll bet a piece of apple goes down good after a long sleep." We each took a step towards each other and I tossed another piece. The brown cub scampered down from his tree to get in on the free food, so I alternately tossed pieces to each of them. Soon we drew closer and closer: 10 yards, 8 yards, 7, 6, 5 yards, and then we were only 3 yards apart from each other. She took a tentative step closer, whereupon I slowly held my arms high and said quietly, "No, no, mama, that is close enough for now." She immediately turned away and stopped at 5 yards. I went to the house for one more apple. By the time I offered the gift of the second apple, I was again very close to her, with the brown cub beside her and the black cub behind me up a tree. Yup, I was between mama and her cub, her body language as relaxed as mine. Like touching the nose of a whale, a curious wolf following you on a walk, or a moose standing a short distance away, it is a wondrous thing to cross the line of fear of man and beast; to somehow sense that neither party wanted to hurt the other, but each was drawn to the other out of a level of curiosity. Perhaps it was folly to offer a gift to the bear, but it is stored in my memory that all people and all animals carry their own personalities—and sometimes, sometimes, a glimpse of understanding might be had between the two.

Several times over the years cubs have been chased up the very same tree that the hunter is sitting in. They are no respecter of tree; they will scamper up the one closest to them. Needless to say, this can be a little unnerving for the hunter when three little bear cubs are in the same tree as they are, with the sow looking on from below. One time one of my hunters had the cubs of two different sows up in trees by him—one sow had two cubs up a poplar tree about 20 yards from him, and the other had two cubs up the very same spruce tree that was part of the stand he sat in. Another time, while walking in to the tree stand with the hunter, we were bluff charged by a bear, an unnerving experience that can help one to stay awake and alert. The strange thing was that even though I suspected it was a sow that had cubs right close by, we could not see any in the treetops. It was not until I picked up the hunter just before dark that I was to learn that two bear cubs were higher up in the very same tree that supported the tree stand. They were up in the tree all along as the hunter climbed into the stand and I passed up his bow and arrows to him! Nope, he did not fall asleep or even get drowsy that evening, nor did he film this free movie. He was too nervous to move and to turn on his video camera, choosing to keep his hands on his bow and arrow in case mama bear might climb the tree.

Though some of these cub-in-same-tree-encounters were quite frightful to the hunters, all of them ended up without injury to both man and beast. However, there are no guarantees. If this same scenario were to happen to a hunter with grizzly bear cubs, I would suggest perhaps a more urgent prayer. Remember, it makes no difference at all, I repeat, no difference at all to say to a bear, "Oh, %#@*!" versus "Oh, banana peels!" as beasts like bears will most likely be looking at your body language and all that it resonates, which in some ways is kinda like our Creator who sees all. So keep in mind that our Creator knows well our body language before we even pray.

Earlier in the season I phoned my friend Bob who was coming on yet another "once in a lifetime hunt" (his 16th year in a row) to ask him what he thought of having a dog in camp. He said he had no problem as long as it was not a whiney dog that had to come in the boat every time we left camp to hunt or fish. I assured him that Trixie was far from that. I told Bob that it was probable there would be bears wandering around my trapline camp every day during the springtime, and that they would chew up gear, grub boxes, and the small freezer plugged into a small Honda generator, so a good bear dog would come in mighty handy. Indeed, there do be bears that walk these woods.

And so it was decided that Trixie was to join the group of five guys and myself who made up the hunt of '05. She and Robert seemed to thoroughly enjoy the flight just below the stratus cloud layer, as they stared at the moving ground below. Not to be deterred by this high-risk private pilot, Robert had decided to travel with me in my homebuilt Murphy Rebel rather than with the rest of the gang and gear which were flown out from the community of Snow Lake by the large Norseman. Canada geese and snow geese were spotted moving in their northerly formations in the cool morning air. After a one-hour flight into the strong northeast head winds, Tulabi Lake was in sight. The landing was smooth and uneventful, unlike the events to follow.

I taxied on the water to the camp area and cut the engine to coast towards the dock. Upon opening my window, I heard the unmistakable sounds from behind me of gear toppling out the window, onto the pontoon, and bouncing into the water. With a quick glance, I saw that a one-gallon pail of homemade cookies had fallen and spilled some of its contents into the water, leaving a trail of cookies on the lake bottom. This trail of cookies would come in quite handy, for all a fellow had to do was to follow this trail to find Robert's camcorder, still floating in its black vinyl case just beyond the cookie trail. A quick glance forward told me that I should have utilized the right rudder pedal sooner as we were heading in a direct collision course with the dock. So, thinking quickly, I made a hasty exit from the plane and quickly leapt forward to reach out with my long arms and brace myself on the dock to try to absorb the shock of impact. My hope was that Robert would become distracted by my concern for his camcorder and forget that I hit the dock with the pontoon, but at this point he had no idea that his camcorder was even in the lake, nor did he have any idea that the camcorder was settling lower and lower. And I hoped that he would understand my rescue of the cookie pail before his camcorder.

"Welcome to Tulabi Lake camp, Robert!" I said with a sense of sinking urgency. "Here, hold the wing for a moment while I go up on shore to flip the canoe over!"

"Well, why don't you just tie up the plane first and then go flip the canoe over?" he answered with curiosity.

"Now look, Robert, I am the outfitter here, the one

who has to make some business decisions from time to time, and I don't think your camcorder will be floating forever," I said while pointing my index finger toward the now barely bobbing black vinyl case.

I do not know if my professional aura was in any way compromised in Robert's eyes by day one of the hunt, but it certainly was eventful. Anyhow, by the time I ran, flipped the old canoe over, dragged it to the lake, and followed the trail of cookies, the camcorder was completely submerged. Let it be safely said that there is not much glory in rescuing a water-logged camcorder that no longer works. Passing the now heavy case to Robert, I asked, "Could you find it in your heart to forgive me by the end of the hunt?"

"We'll see," he answered.

We soon had the plane secured and unloaded. With her feet back on terra firma, Trixie excitedly began barking and running this way and that as her nose directed her, for her nose told of very fresh bear scents. Indeed, the outhouse had been pushed over onto its side, making it a bit of a challenge for someone to use. It is not a large and heavy outhouse, but the long, black hairs told the story that a bear had pushed it over. Trixie's excited barking led me to the far side of the little shed that I had made extra 'bear-proof' last autumn, having nailed on some heavy-duty log siding on the exterior. On an earlier trip I had flown in several sacks of oats, to be used for baiting the bears, and had stored the full bags in this bear-proof shed. But though I had been here only three days prior, there on the east side was a torn off piece of log siding with the nails still in it, and holes chewed through the half-inch plywood that had been behind it. The bear had reached in with its paw and ripped a couple bags of oats open, spilling some of their contents onto the ground. Inspecting the full length of the piece of log siding led me to believe that it was no small bear that had pulled it off, even though there were some smaller tracks of bears mixed in. There were several bears that had been visiting my camp lately, and, judging by all the signs, I was more than glad to have brought along Trixie, who was now in her element of defending this camp from would-be intruders.

I have heard it said that you should not have a dog with you in the bush, for the dog will just bring a bear back to its master. And true, this has happened and will continue to happen from time to time, but cannot our biased opinions be challenged from time to time as well? Will the wolf bring back a bear to its den full of young pups? Indeed, the wolf and the bear have come to an understanding through many, many encounters with each other. Perhaps it is the same with our dogs. If we have taken our dogs from the city to go on one camping trip every three years, how is the dog able to learn the body language of the bear and know its own limitations to overcome its own fear, let alone the owner of the dog who carries the same fear? And so it only makes sense that we will be quick to speak of things that we know not, proclaiming our perceived vast knowledge, which in reality is perhaps only ignorance. I am pleased to have a dog like Trixie in the bush with me, for she has gained confidence with bears from numerous encounters every year. You see, perhaps it is that once a dog recognizes that it can out-maneuver and out-run a bear, it becomes more confident and sees no reason to run back into the arms of its master. (I do not like the word 'master' or 'owner' when describing whom a dog might belong to, but rather it is a working and traveling relationship of teamwork, of which both man and dog benefit.) And so when Trixie chases a bear in the summertime, I will often run with her to see yet another young bear up a tree, a sow with cubs, or an older bear that sometimes holds its ground before slowly loping away, for there are things to be learned when following the scent that a dog follows.

It is true that there are many 'bear experts' to be found amongst the cafés, bars, barbershops and other social clubs that dot our country. Even though I have lived and traveled the bush for all these decades now, I am no expert in bears, but only I seek to ask questions, to read, and to watch what a bear might do, for even bears carry a fear of the unknown.

Speaking of bear experts, one time a fellow told me in great detail of his family's canoe trip. The amount of words and detailed adventures might have indicated that it was a two-month long trip, when in reality it was only a three-mile paddle to an island where they spent one night. He described to me their fearful time of being surrounded by a herd of bears all night long, how these bears swam around the island and made strange noises at them. I asked him if he or his family had actually seen the bears, and if he would imitate the snorting sounds. No, they did not actually see any bears, and he was not very pleased when I said that he was not describing the body language of the black bear, that what he had described was the sounds and body language of a family of otters. Indeed, the fear of the unknown will sometimes prompt us to conjure up wild tales to perhaps justify our own fear, for there is not much glory in discovering that our fears are sometimes caused by our own shadow or a little mouse crawling about during the night.

It is not uncommon for bears to eat their own, especially cubs being killed by a boar and devoured from time to time. Though I have never actually witnessed this, I did see the signs of such an encounter. One autumn, my son Forrest and I were walking down one of the trapline trails along the river, using the chainsaw to clear any deadfall or growth of willows that hung over the trail. There was a light dusting of snow that covered the ground, and it is more than delightful to travel the land of autumn, seeing with human eyes the first visible tracks of squirrels, rabbits, grouse, lynx, marten and a host of creatures that call this land their home; tracks that are always there but are hard to see with the limitation of the human senses. About one mile down the trail, Forrest pointed out a tall jack pine tree to the right of us up a slight rise. The pine tree had been stripped of virtually all its bark, starting from about six feet above the ground to almost the very top, standing out in stark contrast to the other pine trees around it. It was something I had never seen before, so of course we went to check it out.

The pine tree was laced with the black hairs of bears, with the whole of the tree scratched with claw marks from different sized bears. There was not a five-inch square of bark to be seen that was free of claw marks! Every single branch of the pine tree had been chewed off, from the lowest one right up to the last few feet of the treetop. Some of those chewed-off branches were of a full two-inch diameter, sign of a very agitated bear! There was evidence of a couple of cubs and a sow, and of a much larger one, probably a boar. About five yards from the base of the tree was a hollowed out place on the ground, evidence the larger bear had slept and rested there, patiently waiting out the realm of time which would eventually weaken the family of bears up in the pine tree. The signs showed that at least one of the cubs was devoured; the ground was probably hollowed out some by the large boar digging and licking up some remnants of fat and blood. Carefully checking around, Forrest and I counted nine different piles of stool all within eight yards of the pine tree. The stools varied in contents and colour, and a couple of those stools had the hairs of a black bear in it.

Putting together the signs, it appeared to me that this encounter had happened about three or four days prior to our discovery. By now it was October 16, a time when most black bears around here are fattened up by blueberries and such and are in their winter dens. That fall, there had been almost a complete failure of the wild blueberry crop, so it is only natural for the creatures of the land to do what they must to survive, for life wants to live. The most striking thing to me of this whole encounter of fresh and vibrant signs, signs that boldly told of a desperate struggle of survival between the different bears, was that it was quite probable that the cubs and sow were kept up in that jack pine tree for at least 24 hours, perhaps even for two or three days. The signs seemed to portray the work of a very hungry boar that would not have survived the winter without the feasting on one or more of its own kind, a hunger that prompted it to wait under that tree for a very long time. Now really, I'd best be getting on with this hunting story.

The rest of the hunters arrived a couple hours later, and the old Norseman aircraft was once again southward bound, the fading sound of the radial engine reminding us that we were indeed in a quiet part of the Precambrian Shield of Canada. A land of boreal forests that were broken up by endless streams and rivers that entered and drained countless lakes both big and small, most virtually untouched by the hands of mortals.

It is a pleasure for me to be in the bush with a group of hunters who walk about with youthful glee, like little children in a gigantic playground. They can catch a fish whenever they want, sip a cup of hot coffee, or sit in a tree stand for several hours each evening. For some reason my little camp is not filled with macho-type hunters, rather it tends to draw 'real' people. Perhaps it is a valid question to ask at what point a person becomes real? Or does a person also become real, in part, because of our own perception of how we now view people? Whatever the reason, it is more·than pleasurable to spend some time in the bush with these hunters. Frank is a Vietnam vet, with long hair and inner scars, yet he helps me to see that chaos can be brought into some semblance of order, plus he will sometimes catch the biggest and most fish with the cheapest rod and reel of the group. Big John, all 340 pounds of him, with his deep bass voice, is grateful for life and will send me a thank you note after the hunt, plus he can carry double the load of anyone else. Warren talks and laughs easily, and I was honoured that, while a solitary loon called out, he shared a part of his personal dark world as we stood by the fire one night. A world that is hard to see if one is not a part of it, and by the week's end he had given me some insight into what a real person might be. Indeed, Warren caused me to think long and hard about what constitutes a real person. Robert was the youngest of the group, somewhat reserved, yet obviously loved his family back home in Kansas, and I hoped he would not hold it against me for dropping his video camera into the lake. And as always, my friend Bob, and those last three words say it all.

It seems strange to put a price tag on a black bear, a free roaming animal of the forest that respects no political border or party, yet is another commodity in our world of consumption. My clients come to my camp for a certain fee of money; it is not for free, a paradox it would seem. Yet it is the realm of trade that keeps the money flowing and the jobs created, an intriguing nature of supply, demand and hype, an artificial hype that has the power to set a price for a commodity. But as I look around, ask questions and read, I see that all things in this world have a price tag, from mosquitoes to water to humans. In cities we spend large sums to control the mosquito population, mosquitoes that are food for the birds of the air, yet we try to kill them off so that they are not an irritant to us humans. And who would have thought that water could be more expensive than oil? Yet marketers have convinced us to drink bottled water, creating a huge garbage heap of plastic bottles for landfills, or tossed out on the side of the road. The medical professions are powerful, just like the steel workers union or other unions, and so sometimes we become preyed upon by the greed of the high-wage medical economy when we are most vulnerable, when our bodies are sick. Yet we do not die nearly as young as people in Sudan or Ethiopia do, so this tells me that human life is also a commodity. And so societies come together and arranges amongst ourselves an appropriate price tag of such commodities as bears, mosquitoes, oil, water and humans, as the economic time-frame of history allows. Perhaps life is a veritable paradox, a tangled web of life of which we are all a part?

Within 24 hours we had our first bear in camp. I had just left in my boat, the *Dam Hopper*, to drop off some of the hunters at their tree stands. The two guys in camp said that a medium sized bear had come to within 30 yards of the cabin before Trixie rushed to confront it. Apparently the bear did not run off right away as Trixie barked and danced about with much agitation. Young bears will most often take off running when Trixie confronts them and gives chase, but older bears have more experience and confidence to hesitate and call the bluff if they so choose. But with Trixie's persistence and a few yells from the two guys, the bear eventually took off.

I had promised the hunters that we would probably have bears in camp every day, but it took about 24 hours to have the first bear come in. We were having an afternoon nap while Trixie was lying on the porch; she suddenly leaped up with loud barks and started running into the bush. Bob and I quickly put on our shoes and ran after her. We could hear crashing in the bush, the sound of a large bear taking off running, and then it stopped. As I ran into the bush I heard the bear bellow out a windy "Phsssoooff!" towards Trixie. I slowed to a walk to try to catch a glimpse of this bigger bear. I could hear Trixie hopping and dashing and shouting out a few barks as the bear faced her, with the bear mixing in a few more bellows of "Phsssoooff!" while it gnashed its teeth together with clicking noises. When I got to within 60 yards or so, I finally caught a glimpse of the bear as it decided to lumber away at a steady but unhurried pace, confident in its size and strength but eager to leave the sounds of noise and confusion. There is usually a rifle in my arms when I run after Trixie who runs after the bear, and it is a marvel to glimpse, in part, the body language of man and beast, to push beyond the boundary of the fear of the unknown, yet to try to learn and respect the close proximity of the boundary of comfort.

It has taken me long to realize that to bridge a partial understanding of mortal to mortal, or mortal to animal, a bridge can be built easier if one can learn to recognize and challenge, in part, one's own bias that has fooled us into thinking our egos are superior to other thoughts and ideas and body language around us, be it man or beast. So it started to make some kinda sense to me that if a bear cannot speak the English language that I speak, nor can it operate a boat or an airplane, or have a dialogue on politics and religion, it seemed to make sense to me that perhaps I could take the initiative and watch the body language of the bear and learn to imitate some of its reactions, be they of aggression or fear. One time a fellow trapper, Bryan Lundie, had flown out with me to the cabin to call moose for a week. It was a pleasure to walk with this Cree man, to try to see through his eyes as we traveled through the bush, to see what he would be drawn to. His questions and comments were more than intriguing to me. One night as we sat around the table, he asked, "What does a bear see when it looks in the window?" It's questions like these that do not, nor could not, be replied by a quick and straight answer, for they were the kinds of questions that would either be dismissed, or cause one to question and to challenge our own perceived perceptions of life. So I was intrigued to discover that when I was in close proximity of a bear, I could initiate a "Phsssoooff!" sound while clicking my teeth and sometimes have a bear answer in a similar manner. And if I were to back up slowly and increase the distance of our comfort zones, that both of us would tend to relax more.

The intent of this short story was not of a boastful nature of the mighty hunters and their prey, but only to glimpse into the complexities of life of both man and beast. The hunters have enriched my life not only in a monetary sense, but also in the complexities of human nature as we try to find some common denominators through the tangled web of our different lives. For if we point a finger at one segment of life which is a part of the whole, do we not ultimately have to point a finger back at ourselves as well? The hunters have prodded me, and themselves, to learn more about the magnificent animals that we share the planet with. They have prompted me to seek an understanding of the commodities of life and why we place a price tag on them all, commodities such as mosquitoes, water, oil, bears, and humans. They have prompted me to ponder in wonderment the ancient prophesy: "In those days the lion will lie down with the lamb"—in those days the wolf will lie down with the caribou. And if this prophesy will one day come true, it will not come without compassion and understanding.

"We cannot with the mind understand the spirit, because the spirit alone gives the power of understanding to the mind."

—Brihadaranyaka Upanishad 2.4.14 and 3.7.23

Springtime

Ever so perceptibly it comes, like the murmurs of many prayers making the sound of a river that travels powerfully on a unified course. To a bystander it may be difficult to see this river other than a surging mass of water, but the Creator has known each of the individual droplets from the very source whence they came. Even from the heights of a mountaintop where the snow had accumulated year upon year, the weight of it all pressing into ice and forming glaciers that took numerous years to be forced down by gravity and the pressure of mass, the Creator had not forgotten those droplets of water. Eventually the glacier was forced down to an elevation that was conducive for melting, releasing the individual water droplets that had been frozen for a thousand years or more. And all of these droplets, together with the melting snows, spring rains, morning dews, and even the minute droplets coming forth from the breath of mortals, converged together to form swollen creeks and rushing rivers like the voices of many prayers.

Springtime in the North is a time of water in liquid form, pulsing and moving and lapping with celebration. The ice has finally melted from the shallow bay and it is soon filled with the sounds of ducks, geese and loons. These migrants have landed on the water not five or six days after the ice had left, but on the very same day, clapping their wings, honking, quacking, calling, echoing together in chorus the ancient sounds of spring that promise new life. An eagerness of the mating ritual permeates the land with song.

There is another sound that begins in the shallow bay as soon as the ice leaves the bay but not necessarily the lake: the croak of a little amphibian. From the kayak my ears perk up to the lone sound. Within the hour there are several more croaks coming from the quickly awakening frogs. The lengthening days of the spring sun bestows its gift of heat to the landscape which changes its clothing from winter to spring, for winter clothing is no longer appropriate. And so the winter layers are shed piece by piece, like lovers preparing to embrace, allowing the spring sun to penetrate deeper and deeper.

The frogs are awakening on the same spring day that my wooden paddle propels the kayak slowly forward. Sometimes there are days that must be paddled slowly, bit by bit, to soak in the wonders of the land. If I paddled at a hurried pace, my senses would probably not perceive the growing chorus of frogs. And so there is always a trade-off in life, and I raise my paddle in thanks to my Creator for giving me the breath of life that I might live and move and have my being upon the spring waters when the frogs are awakening. Every year I am astounded that by the time the spring sun begins to set on the first day of the frogs' awakening, there is now a roar of croaking. So many frogs have come awake from their long winter's sleep, that there are no individual frogs to be heard anymore, but only the echoing voice of a thousand frogs all at once, as if not a single one of them wants to be left out of the meaningful chorus. And so my soul is made well on this spring day from the sounds of little amphibians.

Shall a man bore you with such details of the seasons, you who are busy in the midst of pursuing commerce and trade? Will the first croak of a little frog have any meaning whatsoever? We pursue commerce and trade in order to provide shelter and food. But even when we have shelter and food, we now pursue commerce and trade for more food and larger shelters and investments, with the goal that perhaps one day we can take life easy and smell the roses and listen to the frogs. And if we are caught up in the pursuit of commerce and trade, we may wake up one day to find that we are now too old and tired or dead to do the things in life that we had so elusively searched for, pursuing goals in life that were always there from the beginning. But what I do know is that it is never too late to kneel down to smell a rose or listen to the sounds of spring.

The last big pan of ice is being pushed along by a northeast wind. The snow had covered the land deep and, coupled by an early warm spell, the lake level rose quickly. In years like these when the water level rises quickly, the ice can move easily along and destroy docks or cabins that have been built too close to the water's edge, reminders to us of the absolute power of nature's seasons.

There is a ten-foot wide lead in the large cake of ice, and so I paddle the kayak through this inviting new trail of water that appears to have been made for no other reason than to be followed. Many years of ice travel can break down the wall of fear of the unknown. Piece by piece, the unknowns of life become, in part, more known, and so paddling amid the ice has been a joy and wonder to me. The close calls of youth have helped to forge reminders of how dangerous ice can be, but should the realm of ice be feared just because the infallibility of youth has been challenged? No, have the freedom to travel amongst the ice, but travel well, for there are marvels to experience within the world of the spring ice.

After paddling about 400 yards, I notice that the lead in the ice is beginning to close rather quickly, so quickly that I have no choice but to rock the kayak from side to side as the ice closes in, squeezing the kayak up onto a solid cake of ice. The plastic kayak slides up with ease, atop a world of solid ice that was once a black open lead of water. Up ahead about 200 yards the open expanse of water beckons. I put one foot out of the kayak and, stepping lightly and testing the ice beneath me, with one foot on the ice and the other in the kayak, I propel the craft forward in a skating motion with a speed of probably 8 mph. The kayak slides noisily and effortlessly upon the candled ice, and, when I am within 20 yards of open water, I sit back down in the seat of the kayak, helping the forward momentum along by pushing with my hands on the ice. The last 5 yards of ice breaks easily as the kayak slips into the open water. Candled ice is ice to watch out for; it bears the mark of spring ice. Melting temperatures have caused the winter ice to form vertical fractures throughout. When this ice breaks off at the edges of open water it breaks into long, thin pieces, like long icicles on the edge of a cabin roof, as long as the ice is thick. Candled ice is dangerous to fall through, because the edges keep shattering as you try to extricate yourself. Many a moose or caribou has fallen prey from breaking through candled ice.

The following day is sunny with a crisp northeast wind moving the last remnants of ice pans along. Shall a man stand by the shore to watch this all when he could paddle out and drift with the last of the ice instead? The passion of celebrating the open water is too great to be missed, so I paddle the kayak to the far end of the lake to come around on the upwind side of the drifting floe. There are ducks that are flying overhead, appearing delighted with all the available open water.

With strong thrusts of the paddle, the kayak slides up onto the drifting floe and there I rest, drifting with the power of the ice. Is it an evil thing for a man to rest on an ice floe with a cup of coffee in his hand? The speed of travel is not great, certainly much slower than an osprey or a Boeing 737, perhaps 1 mph, but there are many things in life that cannot be measured by speed alone. Or did you think that miles per hour can measure the soul of humankind?

The speed of the last remnants of drifting ice is sufficient to fill my soul with the sounds and sights of succulent memory, both old and new. Time has come to a standstill, time just is. It is indeed a sensuous journey, surrounded by the clashing and tinkling of the candled ice that produces the sound of a thousand chandeliers. Perhaps that is why the ice of the springtime becomes candled, for no other reason than to be able to celebrate with unparalleled music? Whatever the reason, it has not been a wasted day to travel along with the last remnants of drifting ice. There are two sets of mallard ducks and three seagulls that have shared the journey with me, sitting on the ice about 50 yards on either side of me. They could have rested in the freshly open waters, but no, they chose to travel with me upon the drifting ice. As we drift alongside the edge of an island, the ice flows in its chaotic order as if there were streams entering a river—there is a sense of order to it all. The ice pushes hard against the shore, tumbling rocks and sticks, pushing over clumps of willows, and I am mesmerized by the season.

Will celebration be traded for commerce and trade? And if this is a reasonable question, is it not true that there is more than one way to measure progress? Will the sands of time see us ever chasing, ever pursuing the distant rainbow that holds no pot of gold? Has commerce and trade deluded us with illusions that dampen our senses to see the beauty that is all about? Perhaps it is reasonable to suggest again that miles per hour cannot measure the soul of humankind.

The following morning there is no ice to be seen, save the piles that have been pushed up on the southwest shoreline. It takes a moment to realize the drastic change. My senses notice the change but have not articulated it yet, awakening as from a sleepy dream. There are the sounds of yesterday, today, and tomorrow, the lapping of the waves against the shore. It was only seven months ago that I heard this same sound, just before a calm, cold night froze the water from shore to shore. It is the sound of lapping water that brings proof that spring is indeed here; one season heightening the appreciation for the next.

There is something else I will tell you about, with the hope that this page will not become too dreary and boring for you. It is later in the same day that the lake was clear of ice that I paddled to the far shallow bay, the same bay that I have paddled to for decades just after the ice leaves. There is a knowing that certain species of fish will spawn at their appointed seasons, and so it is with northern pike that spawn in the shallow, weedy portions of the lake. What I have known for many years is that there do be large pike in these shallow bays. I paddle slowly, hugging the shoreline, every second or third stroke of the paddle causing swirls and splashes as the pike swim away from me. Numerous times there are very large swooshes and splashes of water, swooshes and splashes that are large enough to rock my little kayak, the movements of water that can only come from one thing: monstrous northern pike. When my heart stops skipping and I no longer jolt with fright and appreciation is when I will cease this experience of watching the monstrous pike in the spawn.

There is a small black bear ambling along the shoreline, oblivious to my approach and the splashes of the pike. From a short distance of only 15 yards, I say softly to the bear, "Welcome to spring!" It looks up quickly, stares for a few seconds, and then turns away crashing through the bush.

Paddling back to camp, I notice that there is very little

ice left on shore from the warm, sunny and windy day. I am in the sacred cathedral of which there is none more so. There are angels watching with delight. 'In Spirit and in Truth' have I sought from this day; even a scoundrel such as I have caught a glimpse. All the little drops of moisture that had been frozen for so long, the compacted snowflakes, have become one with the lakes and streams and rivers, heading back to the oceans from whence they came. It is like a journey of many prayers, of many little water droplets that know their Source. And their journey was not in vain…

"No one is born hating another person because of the color of his skin, or his background, or his religion. People must learn to hate, and if they can learn to hate, they can be taught to love, for love comes more naturally to the human heart than its opposite."

—Nelson Mandela
Long Walk to Freedom

Who is My Neighbour?

Trixie, my dog, has been with me on many canoe trips; we've slept outside together on numerous occasions of every year; she had a serious encounter with a large bull moose one autumn so she has been shy of confronting moose since then. She is not overly bold in confronting wolves, and that is fair enough for a 45-pound dog. But she has yet to back down from any bear, and she has numerous encounters every year; several times I've run with her to watch the reaction of the bear (or bears, sow and cubs) to her. We have moose hunted on our fly-out trapline together, just her and myself. She is aloof and often plays 'hard to get', but there is no dog more loyal than she. She will curl up beside me occasionally, on her terms, not mine. For whatever reason in life we are sometimes persuaded to choose, and I could not have asked for a better dog than Trixie.

Over the years I have had numerous encounters with wolves, their haunting chorus having the capacity to reach deep into my soul, our souls. It seems to me sometimes that perhaps wolves, like the common loon, have such a haunting and alluring cry that the vibration of the sound itself might carry the code to unlock the recesses of the wilderness within our souls. The wolves themselves do not live in a wilderness land, for the wolves live in a land that the Creator has made for them which provides such things as voles, mice, beaver, caribou, moose, and the fresh green grasses to nibble on in the springtime to sustain them. It is a sometimes bountiful land of plenty, and a sometimes desperate land of starvation that they live in; but through it all, for thousands of years, they have survived and survived well in the lands that have not been converted into concrete and steel. It is for this reason that, for me, the term 'wilderness' might more aptly apply to the lands of concrete and steel, the places that have lessened the possibility for the green grasses to grow to provide the nutrients for insects, voles, rabbits and wolves, and clean water to drink.

My neighbour, the wolf, came again to visit us in January of 2008. It was a lone wolf, black, medium sized. Wolves have many times over the years come within 50 yards of our camp. On three different occasions I have seen a lone wolf come nose to nose with one of my dogs. On another occasion I found only the head of a Siberian husky attached to its chain, all that was left from a pack of wolves that came in during the night. It is not uncommon for a wolf or a pack of wolves to kill and devour dogs, or to eat their own on occasion, for they too carry the blood and breath of life, the desire to eat and to live. A well-fed wolf can better afford to play than a hungry wolf—no different from humans. It is for that reason that, for me, to see a wolf come nose to nose with one of my dogs is a very special, almost sacred moment—as if catching a glimpse of prophetic words that tell of the day that the lion might lie down with the lamb.

We first noticed our new neighbour, the lone black wolf, when our two dogs started barking on an early morning at the beginning of January. The wolf did not go away, so Cindy brought our dogs inside so she could sleep without the noise of defensive barking. Around 6:00 a.m. I let the dogs outside as I stepped out the door for my morning pee, at which time they immediately carried on their barking.

At the first hint of daylight Cindy spotted the wolf curled up on the ice about 150 yards away from camp. Trixie would edge closer to the wolf than our smaller dog would. I put my parka on and stepped outside with my rifle, not to shoot, but only as a natural precaution as I watched Trixie and the wolf. They were playing with each other; my wife and son also saw it. The wolf would gallop away with Trixie chasing it, and then the wolf would stop and run back towards Trixie who would run back towards camp. The first time we saw the wolf chase after Trixie in the deep snow we saw how effortless it was for the wolf to gain on Trixie's much shorter legs. As I watched the wolf gain ground I thought to myself, "What the…!", put a shell in the chamber and held the scope on the wolf. That wolf caught right up to Trixie and playfully nipped her; she nipped back and the wolf stopped. They repeated this game several times.

A couple days later my neighbour, the wolf, returned. The dogs had been doing their similar body language of barking during the night, so we knew it was back. At first light I strapped on my snowshoes and, with rifle in hand, started off to walk my secret trail across the frozen bay some 450 yards. I had just stepped onto the ice when I noticed the wolf stand up from where it had been lying some 200 yards from me. It started trotting towards the south as I walked, stopping at the point of the small island when I too stopped. Then something strange happened—it was not a new movement that my neighbour, the wolf, had made, but it was something that I have never seen before in the wild: the wolf wagged its tail a couple of times while looking right at me as it sat down 150 yards away. Needless to say I was quite dumbfounded. My new neighbour had, in its own way, waved at me. I smiled back and continued snowshoeing across the bay.

After passing by the tip of the island, there came the wolf trotting along with me about 150 yards away. I stopped, it stopped and then sat down. I again continued snowshoeing and, just before entering the bush, I stopped once more. The wolf also stopped and sat down. "Who are you, and what is your name?" I shouted to the wolf. It remained quiet. As soon as I started walking, the wolf got up and also walked into the bush.

All things in life are curious in their own right. To have a wolf follow from a distance is not unusual, especially at night. Two years ago a small pack had followed me while I snowshoed alone in the dark with only an axe in my hand. From the point where they started howling they never quit, edging closer and closer, spreading out and circling, herding me perhaps to instill panic. It was a night that I knew fear, but the outcome of it all was that I was left with, what was for me, a profound spiritual encounter.

The lone wolf that had now entered the bush with me had a body language that left me with little fear, but rather elation and a sense of awe; a timber wolf had actually wagged its tail at me! It was like touching the nose of a whale, or standing fifteen yards from a curious black bear that meant no harm; like catching a glimpse of the prophetic vision that in those days the lion will lie down with the lamb.

If I had a sense of smell as good as my neighbour the wolf does, my fellow mortals might think that I possessed great spiritual powers, for it has been reported that certain dogs have been trained to recognize certain types of cancer within people and communicate this to their handlers. But I saw that our Creator had given different strengths and weaknesses to all of the creatures of the land and the sea and the air.

It was for the wolf to smell in a much more profound way than a human ever could in this world, but it was for the human to be able to do such things as build a fire or a log cabin, to use a boat, a plane, a rifle or a pen.

In the back of my mind I knew that animals such as wolves have been known to lure dogs away from a camp and then kill and eat them, for it is only natural to eat that we might live. And I knew that it was entirely possible for a well-fed animal to be able to play, and a starving animal to push the boundaries to kill and to eat, with their own species or with other species. My old hometown friend, Ron Isaak, had written recently and told me of his personal interest in wolf and human encounters, which he has experienced himself on some of his hunting trips over the years. After writing to him about one of my encounters, he responded, "I don't know what their behaviour at those moments were dictating, possibly hunting, possibly practicing without the intentions of a fatal end, for I believe they do this often or sometimes. In any case sometimes it also seems that they like to travel with other creatures as well, and show little or no fear that their presence is known or waiting for a reaction."

It was about ten days after we saw our new neighbour the wolf appear to be playing with Trixie that I came home from a trip to town around 9:00 p.m. There was plenty of moonlight upon the land, and as I stepped out of the vehicle there on the ice was the black wolf about 150 yards away. It had ahold of something which, as I listened, sounded like the high-pitched screams of a dying rabbit, the cries of a creature that did not want to die as it called out into the cold night air, for it only makes sense sometimes to cry out to seek life. I noticed our small dog, but did not see Trixie. A feeling of dread began to fill my being as I rushed into the house. "Is Trixie in here?" I yelled to Cindy. "No," she answered, unaware of the scene playing out on the ice. I rushed to the back room to grab my rifle and threw a shell in as I hurried back outside, and then shot just over the head of the wolf. The wolf immediately released its grip and took off. Trixie rose to her feet and staggered towards me with jerky movements for about 20 yards, then collapsed. My son, Forrest, and I ran out to her. Forrest carried her to the house and set her down on the floor beside the woodstove. She was, of course, in shock, with a small patch of blood on her right rear leg and a bloodied neck. There was no massive bleeding, so we knew that no major arteries had been severed, but the damage of a crushed neck would remain to be seen.

I slept beside her on the floor that night, not knowing if she would make it, stroking her body from time to time as she softly whined in pain. During the wee hours of the morning she quieted down, so much so that several times I reached over and carefully listened to make sure she was still breathing. It was not for me to will her to keep breathing, it was only my selfish hope. She did make it through the night, barely moving her body.

First thing the next morning Cindy and I drove 85 miles to bring her to a vet. Over all the years we have had our many dogs, we have never had a habit of bringing them in for such things as needles or grooming or cuts or worms. Once for porcupine quills in one of our husky dog's face, and once for a large protruding cancerous growth, other than that they have run free. Yet Trixie was in such a state that I did not know if she would survive without a little help, perhaps an intravenous or a shot of medication. I would not bring a companion like Trixie in to be put down; I would let no stranger put her down but would play the role of executioner myself as I have in the past. And so here we were, leaving Trixie at the vet's office for two nights, with a $600 bill resulting. This same amount of money might have kept 20 children alive for one year in places like in Africa—but such is the emotional bond sometimes between man and beast.

It has been almost two weeks now since our new

neighbour the wolf attacked Trixie. She has remained inside the house, with painkillers and antibiotics, healing herself. Her leg movements are no longer jerky and spasmodic, only her head still hangs down from swelling and pain, but she is pulling through. Just yesterday I saw her run a short distance, bark and hold her head up momentarily, and then lie down and curl up on the snow. It amazes me how the body can sometimes repair itself. She survived the attack because the wolf had bitten down on the back of her neck where her spine protected her somewhat, and not the front where she is more vulnerable, holding her in that position for at least two minutes. Had it been the front of her neck, her larynx and esophagus would have been crushed and prevented her from calling out her death cry to alert me. There were no tears in her skin, only puncture and crush wounds. Though there could well be, I personally know of no other dog that has survived the jaws of death from a wolf's grip upon the neck; Trixie is one dog who can boast of it.

So now I am left with some inner turmoil—my new neighbour the wolf had actually wagged its tail at me only a few weeks ago. Perhaps the lone wolf was kicked out of a pack, perhaps its other family members were killed by a hunter or snared by a trapper or hit by a truck, or perhaps it came from a small pack that dared to pick a fight with a large bull moose during the autumn rut and it alone survived. Who knows, but whatever the reason, it is known that a lone wolf can have a tough time trying to survive by itself. It, like all other forms of life, seeks to eat and to live—whether vegetarian or carnivorous or a little bit of both, it is the way our Creator has made it to be.

The wolf continues at the time of these penned words to come within close range of our camp in the dark. If I see my new neighbour within 150 yard of me again, or if what more likely will happen is that my dogs alert me to its presence, I will shoot it. It will not be a shooting of revenge, not at all, it will be a shooting because I have chosen one life form over another, both of which desires to eat and to live because our Creator has made it to be that way. I have chosen one over the other merely because of emotions—my emotional attachment to Trixie. And that is the dilemma for me that has given me this inner turmoil. And so, after I sit beside a fire on a cold winter day to spread the smoky perfume upon my clothing and to embrace its cheery warmth upon my body, I sometimes argue with God. *Why did You create us in such a way that we might love our own children more than other children? Is it because of a mere electrical impulse of emotion or a biological alignment of DNA? What greater right do my own children have to life in this world than the children who might die of starvation in poor countries as in Africa? Do You sometimes play a game of chess with us mortals in letting us merely think that we can think?*

I do not expect a bold audible answer from the God of the ages, but, little by little, a sometimes chaotic and tangled web of life makes more and more sense. Who indeed is my neighbour, or what is a great neighbour? Why do we choose to love our own children more than strangers sometimes, oftentimes? To pay the money for piano lessons to give them a 'better chance at life', while the same monies might keep 20 children from Africa alive for a year? Why do we sometimes care more for our own circle of friends, whether politically or religiously, more than other groups? Why do we sometimes care more for our own household rather than our neighbour's, or the flag that we might fly and less so for other flags? Alas, this is mine, yours, and humanity's sometimes difficult dilemma. And so, for whatever reason, we choose.

I just wanted you to know that in my heart I know that Trixie does not deserve any more chance at life than my new neighbour the wolf does, the same neighbour that wagged its tail at me. Out of my emotional attachment and love for my dog Trixie, I will choose her over my new neighbour, and it is my hope that my neighbour might move away before I might have the chance to shoot. This is my dilemma and flaw, if it is a flaw, and I suspect that my Creator will forgive me and us for being so pathetically human in the choices we sometimes make.

It took a full month before Trixie would go for a short walk. I saw the wolf three months after the attack while walking with Trixie. It started running away from 90 yards when I called out to it, "I can see you!" The wolf immediately stopped at about 110 yards and turned to look back. Once more I shouted, "I can see you. What do you want?" and with that we carried on with our walk. Five months have passed now, and Trixie has healed well.

Something else happened that I thought worthwhile to write. It was in early June that a relative with a couple of her friends stopped by. She and her boyfriend are Cree people with strong traditional beliefs, medicine people who harvest various things from the land. I was telling her boyfriend about the dilemma I had with the wolf and Trixie, to listen to his reaction and how he might perceive it. He told me to drop a pinch of tobacco in the lake and make a prayer to the wolf and to the Creator, and then he said, "You will hear a call." After the tea was finished and they were about to leave, he said to me once again to drop a little bit of tobacco into the water, say a prayer to the wolf and "You will hear a call." They were just about to drive away when he got back out of the truck, walked up to me with an open pouch of tobacco and gave me a small handful, which I promptly put into my shirt pocket.

It was only about nine hours later that I rose out of bed at 6:00 a.m. and went to my kayak with a mug of coffee to paddle to a bay a half mile away to listen to the wonders of a new day. As soon as I paddled to the bay close beside the loon's nest, I placed a pinch of tobacco into my hand with the intent of dropping it upon the water's surface as I talked with my

Creator. With the sometimes difficult chasm of bridging cultures, it was not within me to say a prayer to an animal such as a wolf, and it is my folly if it is folly. But I would hold the gift of tobacco in my hand and say a prayer to my Creator. Yet, just as soon as I began a little prayer, something strange happened: I heard the call of a calf moose, once, and then twice more from about 150 yards away! I paddled closer and called out a soft calf call myself. The cow and calf moose came boldly to the edge of the lake towards my call and stopped about 60 yards away. Something profound had happened, and in my heart I knew it was so. I rarely hear the call of the moose in the summer, especially from a land that is not a high-density moose area. But it was twice that the Cree medicine man, who carries the scars on his chest from the Sundance, had said to me these words: You will hear a call. The calf had been right beside its mother each time it called, so what then, I wondered, would be the reason for it to call out at the start of a prayer? What had happened was no mere coincidence, and I knew profoundly once again that our Creator is not dead, and that a sense of meaning had been pieced together for me from Trixie and my neighbour the wolf and the dilemma within me during the past winter.

High-Risk Private Pilot

I suppose that we are all of us a little bit of this and a little bit of that. Might as well call myself a pilot since, technically, I have flown for about 22 years already. I have not really logged too many hours of flight, about 1700 hours at the time of this story, enough to maintain my reputation as a high-risk private pilot. It only makes sense that one may not be as proficient at something if one works at it part-time compared to someone who works at something more on a full-time basis. And so I believe that I will be able to maintain my reputation as a high-risk private pilot until the day I die, or my license is taken away, or a strong wind flips my plane over.

One time there was this old-time pilot who dropped in for a cup of tea. He had about 34,000 hours of flight time under his belt at that time, a pilot that had flown more full-time for a living, so I could only conclude that he must be a lower-risk commercial pilot, at least for awhile. This old pilot had a habit of teasing other pilots such as myself, or perhaps the demeanor that I exuded prompted him to tease me a little bit. Can't say as I am intimidated by a little bit of humour, but perhaps I was naïve enough to believe that one who can give out teasing can also handle some teasing. Guess my social skills needed some more fine-tuning? His comment was something like, "You blankity blank outfitter-pilots who can't even fly think you own the country." I admit he had a point there. I am a blankity blank, and an outfitter, and I can't fly very well, but I sure don't own the country, for who would be foolish enough to think that they could own a rock or a tree? Anyhow, I looked back at this old pilot, who I thoroughly enjoy visiting with, and said, "Here be a riddle for you. It is indeed true that I am a high-risk private pilot and will be to the day that I die, but do you know what will happen? You yourself will turn into such an extremely high-risk commercial pilot that they will not only force you to retire, but they will also take away your license for good. This, of course, will make me a safer pilot than you for a couple of years until my license is also taken from me due to senility and old age and such." This riddle was not met with much humour. I never did have much in the way of social skills, but he has not teased me much about flying since that day.

I don't really have much in the way of adventure stories for you readers what with only 1700 hours, but they were certainly adventurous for me. You see, it don't matter if one is a private or commercial pilot, whether one flies a certified aircraft or a homebuilt aircraft, as the same laws of physics are at work with such things as gravity and the variation of air particles, moisture, temperature, the wing-lift capacity of the aircraft, and the various personalities of the pilots in control. Come to think of it, there ain't many books on the market that tell of the incredible adventures of an airline pilot with 30,000 hours that hauls hundreds of people at a time. "The giant aircraft cruised along on auto-pilot at 42,000 feet above sea level. The stewardess knocked on the pilots' door to bring them a cup of coffee as the chief pilot turned the cabin temperature down. He yawned and discussed the merits of dual-navigation with the co-pilot. The passengers were kept occupied by various movies, food and drink, giving extra attention to the first-class passengers compared to those in second-class. Eight hours later it was time to begin a descent. The aircraft landed without incident at Tokyo International Airport. The End." It only makes some kinda sense to me that a compelling adventure story is not necessarily bettered by a much larger, more comfortable and faster aircraft with pilots of greater hours of flight time.

I got my flying license in 1986 and found a Cessna 180 with floats and skis later that year. This hunk of aluminum with a 225 h.p. engine was merely a tool that I used for staking mining claims, cutting grid lines, flying my tent camps around over the years with a couple of men during the winter months on skis, and accessing our remote trapline and wild rice camps in the summertime. It might have seemed strange to some to see a $40,000 aircraft (its value at the time) tied up beside a $2,000 home—a little log cabin that I had built which Cindy and I lived in.

I remember the first glassy-water landing I made with the Cessna 180. My friend Barry had a couple sacks of wild rice seed that he wanted to test-seed on a remote lake. The sun was dropping low on the horizon as the floats contacted the water. As soon as the plane began slowing I realized that the low muskeg shoreline we were heading towards was kinda closer than I thought, which prompted me to turn the engine off completely. Yes, yes, I just turned the key off that time instead of pulling the mixture-lean knob, which I had been taught to do, because the shoreline was appearing quite quickly. Anyhow, the plane dropped from the step and kinda ran up against the soft muskeg at about 10 mph. Barry kinda looked at me with wide brown eyes that could not hide the start of his snicker. I looked at him rather professionally, like we had been taught to do, and told him that there was not much sense taxiing around the lake since this was the very bay and outlet that he wanted to test the wild rice seed in. He merely snickered at my attempt at professionalism, including the professional way that we exited the plane and pushed it off the soft edge of the muskeg. We dropped the bags of wild rice into the water to be seeded at a later date and, since there was no damage to the floats, judged it all in all a job well done.

Everything in life has its learning curve, and all of us must start from somewhere. It was in my first year of ski flying that the waning winter sun found me and three men flying to a remote lake about 80 miles to the southwest of where we were based. The lakes around home were still snow covered, but as we flew south the lakes began to gleam with the sheen of smooth ice. Now it is only natural for a plane to point into the wind like a weather vane. Wheels, snow and water offer a measure of greater control when landing in a cross wind, but landing on slippery ice with skis gives you little directional control. I had not yet experienced landing on this slippery surface, but soon found that as I landed in the cross wind the plane began to turn sideways as it slowed, while quickly approaching the shoreline. The plane just kept sliding and sliding on the smooth ice, as any idiot would know, coming to a sideways stop within about 10 yards of the shoreline of cattails and marsh. The front passenger looked at me, shook his head and said, "I've parked like this a few times in a car, but this is my first time parking sideways in an airplane!" I assumed that this was obviously a compliment, requiring an experienced and competent driver to perform a stunt like this.

There ain't much sense in telling about how once or twice (I forget which one) the passengers had to sit on a sleeping bag, tent or propane bottle instead of a padded seat with a back rest, so as to maximize the pay load; why that might just incur the wrath of the Department of Transport, or D.O.T. Cindy never lets me forget the time she had to sit on frozen beaver carcasses that we were bringing for bear bait, which I guess didn't help with her motion sickness problem. Of course, I sure do get kinda confused when the military flies around with guns and bombs on board, with open doors on the sides of helicopters and such. Why, that must be kinda dangerous as well?

Life brings change from time to time, and in 1994 I sold the Cessna 180 and bought a kit airplane that came in a 4' x 4' x 12' plywood box. This corporate business decision was merely a way to trim down and manage resources within the realm of 'spend less than you make'. After all, I was no mere C.E.O. but rather the illustrious President of this fine, uh, enterprising business decision, which my wife said was merely the whim of a dreamer. This kit plane, called a Murphy Rebel, was sold as a 1250-hour projected build time, not counting floats. We invited my brother-in-law, who happened to be between jobs at the time, to come live with us and help out on this project. He worked with me for the major portion of the building phase, minus about 350 hours of this and that such as putting the floats together and attaching them to the aircraft. He is a meticulous sort who unloaded and sorted out every single tiny part and checked them each off the list. Let it just be said that if he were to build the plane himself it would have taken about ten years to have it flying, and if I had built it completely myself it would have taken about four months instead of six. Of course, I would have wondered why there were all those totally unnecessary parts left over, which my brother-in-law insisted were integral parts to the machine. I suppose he had a point. As it was, through compromise, it took about six months to have the Rebel almost complete. Then the wild rice harvest time came, and then the approach of winter trapping, and exploration work after New Year's, so the plane had to wait for next season's open water.

By the time I dealt with the floats and struts, building inspectors, etc, this new plane was not in the water until early September of 1995. Wheel flying is of no use to me, so it had to be floats or nothing, as all of my work is in remote fly-in lakes. I chose to install a 160 h.p. Lycoming zero-time engine, which brought the plane to an official gross weight on floats of 1800 pounds. This homebuilt plane is about the same weight and performance of a Piper Super Cub, except that it has much more room inside and would cruise about 15 mph faster.

Some mortals within the hierarchal caste system of flying might say that a homebuilt is not a real airplane, especially if it was thrown together by a non-certified mechanic such as myself, but this folly can be easily disproved. You see, the engineering of the plane and its alloys and materials was done by certified engineers and mechanics and such, all the builder had to do was to throw it together in a fashion that might permit flight. The inspectors throughout the building phase were certified individuals. And, get this, the laws of physics have always been fairly constant—air is air, water is water, wings are wings, gravity is gravity, and personalities are personalities.

A chief mechanic told me one time that the D.O.T. had grounded one of their airplanes simply because he had installed a little trim tab on an aileron, a tiny piece of aluminum that could be physically bent to help correct the aircraft from riding low on one wing, to encourage it to fly more level. This particular aircraft was not intended for outer space or breaking the sound barrier, yet a little tiny trim tab had it grounded. Perhaps the 'safety issues' involved are not as great as the 'ruffled feather issues'? Rules have got to be upheld sometimes, why, there are lawyers and unions and courts and corporations all mixed together with varying personalities. This chief mechanic, by the way, was a fully certified mechanic, which kinda tells me that they are sometimes more limited than a high-risk non-certified mechanic such as myself. I installed a little trim tab on one wing and on the rudder to help encourage my plane to fly straight and level; it is routine for aircraft to have these trim tabs since—yup, that's right—no aircraft is a perfect bird. Though it is true that the home-builder has the freedom to experiment to some degree, it also comes with its hazards of experimentation which can translate into more accidents, which is why I can kinda understand the D.O.T. getting involved from time to time to help promote accountability of safer flying. Wait a minute, does this mean that sometimes we homebuilt aircraft pilots are merely guinea pigs to see what is safe and what is not?

One of the benefits of building your own aircraft is that you can do your own maintenance. Every spring I partic-ularly enjoy flying my homebuilt over the float base near town where my Cessna 180 was serviced for many years, but it was rarely ready to fly until early June since it took a lower prior-ity over the base's own floatplanes. Now I win bets on who will be first on floats in the region, thumbing my nose as I buzz at 50 feet in a friendly, most professional manner the base in town with its frozen bay of ice.

It has been brought to my attention on numerous occa-sions that a fellow should NEVER mix different brands of oil in an engine, as this could cause some unexpected and dire consequences. Okay, I do have to admit to mixing engine oils on numerous occasions over the years in different vehicles that I've owned, and I have yet to have an engine seize up on me. But the caste system of engine oils should not be over-looked. In order to narrow down this variable opinion, I mere-ly asked various mechanics from flying outfits which brand of oil is the best kind of oil. Needless to say, there are as many variables as there is brands of oil, and it only makes sense, as doesn't a brand have to come from somewhere? In my opin-ion, a change of brand of oil also occurs during an oil change if you use a different brand, because it is not possible to drain a hundred percent of the previous oil without taking the engine apart. As to the extreme potential dangers from a pilot mixing different oil brands together, I merely asked a little question. Tell me this: you have to pick up a loved one who needs immediate medical attention, whether on the battlefield or in the bush. You have to fly 150 miles to get back to a doctor, and you notice that the engine oil is low. The only oil available is a different brand than the one you normally use. Do you cancel the flight or, dare I say it, pour in a different brand of oil? After the flight has been safely made, do you carefully mark in the logbook that you used a different brand? Do you insist that whoever owns the flight service, whether yourself or your boss, must take the engine completely apart to search for any possible problems? (Please note possible measure of sarcasm here overlying a quest to seek a measure of uh, truth. Also note possible link between corporations, turf-protection laws, lawyers and insurance companies.)

I had not flown anything for 17 months, from the time I sold the Cessna 180 until the time that this Murphy Rebel was on the water for a test flight, nor did I have any training whatsoever on the Rebel. Needless to say it was kinda intimidating, until one day a fellow stopped by and said he would be willing to take it for the first flight. Since he was a commercial pilot for many years, and had a family as well, this gave me a boost of courage. I kinda figured then that this plane would probably fly. I figured that building an airplane was kinda like building an outhouse. If the outhouse was crooked it would still work just fine, but it might be a little awkward for one to sit sideways 30 degrees to help counter the lean.

You see, the building directions had us raise the wing dihedral by about 2 degrees, or was it 1 degree? The back elevator was to be slanted about 2 degrees or so, and the vertical rudder was to be fitted a half-inch off centre, opposite the direction of the propeller rotation to help counter the thrust, or something like that. The floats had to be attached within a certain balance area of the wing-chord, not to mention that these particular floats I had chosen had never before been flown on a Murphy Rebel model. But it was only a mere three weeks from the time I contacted the D.O.T. (who I found were very efficient and helpful) till the time I followed their directions and got the official okay to fly this plane with this new type of floats.

When I first looked at the four small bolts that held the engine in its place I thought that the engineers had it all wrong, for how could these four little bolts hold a vibrating 160 h.p. engine in place for thousands of hours? And then I started looking at the attach bolts for engines in Cessna 185s and de Havilland Beavers and saw how small they were as well, and I was much comforted. Okay, I've bored some of you readers by now with details, suffice it to say that when I build anything and finish it I usually end with an exclamation of, "Good enough!" The controls would be in my hands for the first flight, and for all of them since then.

The rules of the game state that the pilot of a new homebuilt could not take any passengers with them until twenty-five hours had been flown. This sure did not help to instill confidence in me, but like I said earlier, perhaps we home-builders are in fact just guinea pigs. The rules did not say that a passenger was not allowed on board while merely taxiing a plane on the water, and it so happened that a different brother-in-law was visiting. I casually asked if he was interested in some high-speed taxiing on the water on that fine September day with light northeast winds and 12 degrees Celsius. He quipped back, "Sure!" Really, though, I could see no reason why he should doubt the quality of this plane since he had used my outhouse on numerous occasions and the outhouse had never fallen over when he used it. Like I said earlier, building an airplane is kinda like building an outhouse.

We hopped in the plane and fired her up. After taxiing around the bay until the engine temperature gauge was in the green, I applied power to try to get this hunk of aluminum up on step, meaning the aircraft is going fast enough to be planing the water. We were doing some high speed taxiing at only 1800 rpm into the wind when the plane kinda got airborne.

"Ah, shoot! Sorry about that, Frank."

"That's okay!" he said.

"Well, since we're airborne, do you mind if we do a quick circle and then try to land her?"

"Give 'er!"

After completing a cruise around the lake and moving the controls here and there to try to get a feel for her, I set up for a landing, which of course was much more intimidating to me than a take-off in this brand new plane. With flaps down and power reduced, the plane settled lower and lower into the steady northeast breeze and contacted the water with as smooth a landing as I have ever done—though this may not be saying much. Frank and I looked at each other and grinned.

"Frank, since technically a rule has been kinda broken already, what do you say we try a full-power take-off?"

"Give 'er!"

So I applied full power and that little plane sure jumped on step pretty quick. In a short distance we were airborne and climbed to a mere 50 feet, when the engine suddenly quit. It all happened so fast that there was not even time to say "Ah, shoot!" or even a short prayer. Although I do recall that it was kinda intimidating for me to be flying a new aircraft type and not having flown for the past 17 months, there was a sense of comfort in having a passenger along that I might not die alone. The old training from years ago somehow kicked in automatically: stick forward to maintain airspeed (or in this case to try to increase airspeed since I was just above the stall speed), and flare out just before contacting the water. There was no time for me to check out doohickeys like the airspeed gauge and such, since there was only a couple of seconds from engine failure to contact with water. Anyhow, I somehow fluked out on a smooth and delicate landing, the kind that you don't know when the floats made the transfer from air to water. In my case this fluke is undoubtedly true, as I tend to make many more landings per take-offs, otherwise known as bounces. Why, at one time I was marking down more landings than take-offs in my logbook until I learned that one could only log one landing per take-off.

I looked across at Frank, shrugged my shoulders, re-primed the engine and it fired right up. We taxied back to the dock to do an official investigation, which turned up a simple case of fuel starvation. You see, the wing tanks have about 3 gallons of unusable fuel on each side on level flight. Coupled with a backwards lean on take-off and lacking a minimum 45 minutes reserve of fuel (or perhaps a build flaw on my part that resulted in crooked wings with 4 gallons of unusable fuel in each wing tank), caused an unhappy engine. My fuel gauges are just a length of clear tubing, and I have never forgotten that magical line again.

Other than taking a passenger and lacking a minimum reserve of fuel, no other rules had been broken that day. But this same day had shown that the little bush plane could actually fly. Why the manufacturer had called the plane a Murphy Rebel instead of a Murphy Angel is their corporate decision to make. Though I kinda did wonder, if it was called an Angel would it have prompted me to better follow all of the rules all of the time? For me, if it is possible to mix words: this airplane is a rebel that takes off like a home-sick angel.

Yup, I will be a high-risk private pilot until the day I die. Of course, an advantage of that kind of outlook is that one can only move up. Always did kinda wonder what it was like to fly with the silent wings of an eagle.

"...Brother, you say there is but one way to worship and serve the Great Spirit. If there is but one religion, why do you white people differ so much about it? Why not all agreed, as you can all read the Book?... Brother, we do not wish to destroy your religion or take it from you. We only want to enjoy our own... Brother, we are told that you have been preaching to the white people in this place. These people are our neighbours. We are acquainted with them. We will wait a little while and see what effect your preaching has upon them. If we find it does them good, makes them honest, and less disposed to cheat Indians, we will then consider again of what you have said."

—Red Jacket (Sogoyewapha) 1805
granting an interview to a missionary

Creator's Campfire

A growing strangeness appeared to me, and so I thought it worthwhile to write it—the reader may chuckle or curse or label or find a measure of interest. You see, I became aware that certain things I had written had come true, and as the sequences become bolder and clearer to me, I actually became scared of my pen for a while. It seemed kinda silly to be scared of a mere pen, but I suppose life can be like that sometimes. And so, to help overcome this strange fear of a mere pen, I decided to write about my funeral. And when I had written this story, the fear melted away.

I thought I might as well start thinking about a funeral, what with being 47 years of age at this time, already nine years older than the average lifespan in some African countries. Seems to me that no one is getting out of this world alive, statistics showing that one hundred percent of people will die, so I might as well start planning. Of course, it don't hurt to ask questions and read books to seek to understand how different cultures handle funerals and death and such, I guess.

I heard the words of a wise man echo against the cliff behind our campfire on a cold winter night of a full moon. He told me he had read that if a person had God and books in one's life, that person would not need friends. These words seemed to hold a measure of logic to me, that is if one truly believes that God is very much alive and fully capable of communicating with us, and if one knows how to read. Another time I came across the words: *We read to know we're not alone.* If these words hold a measure of truth, would that not mean that we could have a friend within the format of printed words, as if mere words themselves could somehow take on the form of a real live breathing mortal, a friend that we might somehow, in part, relate to? A friend within the printed word that is by no means perfect; with whom we could discuss ideas without the threat of being rejected for whatever we might be, accepting us as we are? Without heated arguments and belittling comments, but only a common goal to seek a measure of truth? Indeed, such is the paradox. Perhaps a good friend is like a beautiful flower, someone to help sort out and make better a sometimes ugly, chaotic and scarred world. Perhaps we were not designed to be fully alone, whether in life or in death. If we then had God in our life, and a book with printed thoughts that we could somehow relate to, would this not be the same thing then that we might claim not to have a need for— a friend? Does this not ultimately prove that we all of us have a desperate need inside ourselves for genuine friendship, the kind that will not cast us off after discovering all that we might really and truly be? And I strongly suspect that this is what the wise man meant when he spoke the words that echoed from the cliff.

In 1842, a man called Santa Anna, a general and an on-and-off leader of Mexico, had a funeral for his leg that he had lost in battle. He explained to a companion his essential modesty, yet due to the demands of some of the Mexican people and some religious leaders, he consented to have a funeral for his left leg. The solemn procession carried through. Gosh, it kinda makes me wonder if we might find more favour with God by having multiple funerals for various body parts and pieces that we might lose in life. Within a couple years, apparently some sacrilegious hooligans dug up the sacred leg, chopped it into pieces and discarded those smaller pieces onto various garbage piles throughout the city. Gosh, how could such a humble and sacred funeral be so despised by some mortals? How dare those common hooligans defy the clergy who obviously had an in with God, and defy the great humility of their on-and-off leader's left leg! (Please note possible sarcasm here and throughout this story.)

I have read of a king that built a great pyramid with the aid of the sweat and blood of multitudes of slaves. He had it adorned with much gold and jewels and beautiful carvings from talented artisans, and he had the tomb filled with a multitude of items to see him through the next world. I guess the spirits of the next world do not know how to properly outfit certain of us mortals to properly carry on. Gosh, perhaps God just does not get it sometimes! Obviously, commoners, slaves and subjugated people won't need to pack much gear for the next world, since they either won't be there or will only have a low caste role to play.

Sometimes certain funerals are long, drawn-out affairs, with trumpets blaring, clergy robed in their finest, a great fanfare of media coverage, and attended by well-known people. Prestigious gatherings that will obviously give those deceased a prestigious and prominent place in the after life. The wealthy are sometimes buried beside elaborate tombstones, the kind that God obviously favours. *Did you really think that fame and fancy robes and mass media coverage could get us a better spot by our Creator's campfire?*

Sometimes mortals were mummified—embalmed and preserved after the manner of the ancient Egyptians—perhaps to preserve a mortal's body for the after life. Now, I ain't never seen a real mummy, only pictures, especially in *National Geographic* magazine. Why, this magazine has had close-up pictures of the face and body of a mummy unwrapped after the passing of a couple thousand years. It would not be my first guess as to how we might look in the after life, shrunken and dried skin wound tightly around a skeletal body with vacant eye sockets, but I suppose that in God's view beauty is in the eye of the beholder. Could it be that we mortals have been looking for beauty in the wrong places?

The type of coffin we choose for our loved ones will obviously express our love for them, with absolutely no pressure from what the people attending the funeral might think, or casket marketers, or funeral homes. Besides, it seems rather obvious to me that better constructed coffins can better aid us into the next world, as God can obviously spot a sub-standard coffin. As to that notion in ancient scriptures that says we will all have to pass the test of fire by our Creator, this can simply be worked around by constructing a casket of steel, or some kind of alloy that can withstand high temperatures. Of course, our Creator was not too specific as to the temperature of the fire that we will all be refined by. It may bring some comfort to know that this purging fire, which will reveal to us what we really are, may not be a whole lot hotter than the core temperature of the earth. Come to think of it, would this not melt everything except spirit? So much for making a choice to be cremated or not. *Did you really think that spirit is defined by the trappings of funerals?*

Apparently some folks have had their bodies frozen with liquid nitrogen, the cryogenics field. Yes, I can just picture some forklift driver after a few beer accidentally knocking over some containers with frozen bodies in them, perhaps driving over one of the bodies and breaking off its head. He may do his best to put everything back in place, but was unable to find the head. As he stumbles around he mumbles to himself, "Man, that guy is gonna have a hard time getting a-head in life when they thaw him out!" Eventually he finds the head and kinda puts it back in place. Some time later a distraught relative finds out about this inebriated incident and shouts to the forklift driver, "You killed him! You broke his head off! He's dead now!" These are, perhaps, some of the challenges and complications of enlightened science, convincing someone to pay exorbitant sums in order to preserve their body with the hope of bringing them back to life someday, though this method may be out of reach for the masses of humanity of our world. *Did you really think we mortals can buy and freeze-dry spirit?*

It is true that the world plays a game where a person can donate $500 and receive a blue ribbon, $2000 for a silver ribbon, or, if you want a gold ribbon, just donate $10,000. Perhaps a donation of $250,000 can get your name emblazoned on a fancy plaque. Heck, for donating twenty-five million you can even have a university named after yourself! Please note that these games of prestige may be out of reach for the masses of humanity. Also note that there is no rule that says one must have their own name emblazoned on a plaque or university building after paying the according sum; you can put someone else's name on it if you so choose. One could even donate anonymously, but the pressures and vanities are great, very great. In my own warped mind, I cannot separate this from certain historic church practices of granting absolution, a little piece of paper granting forgiveness for a price; or uh, a sin buy-out versus a gold ribbon buy-out. It kinda seems to me that, perhaps, deep inside each one of us craves in some measure a piece of immortality, some meaning beyond the grave. *Did you really think that spirit can be bribed? Did you really think that our Creator is blind to the games that we play?*

Gosh, by now I'm kinda wondering just how much our Creator will take into account pomp and ceremony, robes, titles, certificates and preserved bodies. *Can You really see us for what we truly are, God?*

In light of this all (or in narrow-minded of this all), I guess my preference is that not much money be spent on my own funeral. There is no need to have a high-paid doctor certify whether or not I am dead, as a mid-wife can determine this just as well, and all that is required on a death certificate is a little signature. I don't want to burden anyone with a headstone, or a coffin, or yet another plot of ground. I'd far prefer to be cremated on a bonfire in the bush. This, of course, is based on the assumption that my body is there to be cremated. If my body is lost at sea or to wild animals or a river or war or any other way, then there ain't much sense in cremating something that ain't there. The bonfire would require the attendance of at least one person to actually make the fire and keep an eye on it so as to not start a forest fire; perhaps someone could have one of my canoes in exchange for tending this fire. A simple pulley could be rigged to winch my body to the top of the fire if the single attendee is not strong enough to lift or drag it. *Did you really think that the numbers of people attending a funeral directly defines how much our Creator loves us?*

Local by-laws and such may frown on a do-it-yourself cremation, crowding in, I suppose, on the professional funeral home business and such. If these by-laws are strong enough to dissuade you from a do-it-yourself cremation, you may take my body to a crematorium. However, I ask you to not purchase an urn for my ashes, as things such as these can be yet more marketing opportunities by various organizations to capitalize on the emotional state of those left behind. *Did you really think that a fancier urn would get me a fancier place in heaven? Did you really think that spirit is bettered by an expensive urn?* If you feel you must collect my ashes, just put them in an empty coffee can or wine bottle or something. Fret not about the label on the wine bottle, if there is one, whether showing a cheap wine or an expensive one, for these are just the peer pressures of the living. The ashes can be deposited where the loons sing, the wolves call, and the trees dance to the autumn breeze. *Did you really think that my spirit was in the wine bottle? Did you really think that our Creator pays more attention to a posh funeral rather than to a simple one for some unknown street bum who falls into the river and is never found?*

I know that the realm of where the loons sing, the wolves call, and the trees dance is not the necessary gateway to walk with our Creator, it was only my little realm as I knew it, in part, to be. The world comprises so much more: a great expanse of barren lands (which are not really barren, as the Spirit knows), prairie lands, deserts, jungles with lions and wildebeest, broad oceans and the land of the penguins. If my ashes were dropped in the middle of the ocean or onto the lands where the lions dwell, it still would not, could not, take away that which I am. If I were in some way confused, as I have been at times in the land that I knew helped draw me to my Creator, I would merely reach out again towards the hand of my Creator. Perhaps, then, my wish to have my ashes spread in the land where the loons sing, the wolves call, and the trees dance was merely my insecure way of walking a path of comfort and familiarity. Yet, I did find myself asking along the way, What is the comfortable and familiar path of Spirit? Perhaps, then, those who scatter my ashes would know that they are merely ashes. But the memory of the occasion—the faint breeze upon your face as the trees danced, the haunting call of the loon, the spirit-yearning call of the wolf—perhaps all these things might leave behind codes and patterns that the Spirit of our living God did indeed touch the land and our soul. And perhaps we might know that the faint breeze upon our faces at times may have been the faint breeze of the Great Spirit that tried to prod us to walk with the Creator. And so we only thought we felt alone at those times when we looked in the wrong places, but all along, you see, we were never alone.

It is not our clothing that clothes our spirit. Yet if nakedness makes some uncomfortable, you may clothe me with the type of clothing that I've been most comfortable in: a toque or some kinda cap to cover my balding head, a plaid shirt and a wool mackinaw coat, and a pair of wool pants or jeans. *Did you really think that a suit or tie gets us mortals a better seat in the next world?*

You may use the word *dead*, if you wish, for it is indeed true that my physical body is dead, though I tend to prefer the words *passed on*. *Passed on* tends to portray a more neutral stance of that which we cannot know until we ourselves have faced the realm called death. Here is a riddle: How can we mere mortals prove or disprove that which we simply do not know of those who have passed on? Seems to me that I might now, when I have passed on, have one up on those of you left behind: whether death is a good long sleep which is like the blink of an eye, or an automatic transfer of residence. For now, with the knowing within of the scoundrel that I might be combined with the marvel of the profound Grace of the Creator, I am drawn to my Creator's campfire.

Sometimes we play the game of which cemeteries or graveyards are more prestigious or righteous or civilized than others; a sometimes game of caste and class. Segregated graveyards have been at times a favorite pastime, and sometimes still are. Yet the birds of the air fly about and cast their droppings indiscriminately—on expensive tombstones, a small wooden cross, or a pile of rocks. It is as the poet and politician John James Ingalls proclaimed: "In the democracy of the dead all men at last are equal." *Did you really think that our Creator is so dull? Did you really think that unmarked and unknown graves are of lesser value than graves with prominent tombstones? Did you really think that the One who created all things—the planets and stars and the unfath-*

omable heavens beyond—did you really think that the Great Spirit was blind to the one who died alone, or the graves that have been blasted, plowed over, or flooded over time?

Ultimately, it is not a 'whole' body that makes our spirit whole, whether we have lost a limb in a car accident, our body blown to pieces in a land mine, burnt beyond recognition in a house fire, or devoured by wild beasts. *Did you really think that our Creator would not remember us for what we are?* Or someone who chooses, in the despair of the moment, to take their own life. *Did you really think that our Creator did not know of their despair that persuaded them to take such action?*

You see, though I was distracted by much in life (as we all are), in my heart I realized a growing awareness that my Creator could hear my chatting and my pleas and my folly. For how could our Creator align the planets, place the stars beyond measure, set up just the right conditions on Earth to allow us to live and move and have our being, create the oceans and fish and birds and mammals and reptiles and insects and micro organisms, yet be so dull and unintelligent as to not hear the voice of a mere mortal? What really is it that we have strived for in life? What is the meaning of the funeral ritual we might choose compared to the meaning of how we might lead our individual lives—living our lives within plain view of the Great Spirit who knows us within and without? What is it that might be of value?

What mere mortal has known the full mind of God? To move some of the chess pieces of life and to ask questions can sometimes have us in a bit of a quandary, certainly for myself anyway. If one was to ask a simple question such as: "What happens to young children and babies when they die, or the death of the yet unborn through abortion?" For those who believe in some kinda heaven, it is only natural to believe that our Creator would welcome these youngsters. After all, what kind of god would send innocent children into nothingness or the pits of hell? What mortal would dare say otherwise while leading a funeral or memorial service? Will a mere piece of paper that spells the word *baptized* have the power to separate the saved, the damned, or place them in limbo? If this all be true, why was I and the rest of humanity not baptized, then aborted or killed off at a young age so as to ensure our spot in heaven, instead of having to play the games of careers, politics, religions of the right and the left and every caste in between—and the supposed choice of heaven or hell? If this is all it takes to get to heaven, then let us baptize or kill off all of our children at a young age to ensure their eligibility. Whether or not one believes that a fetus is a real person, is it not scientifically correct to say that a fetus is an expression and form of life—the molding of cells? If, as some might believe, the fetus is a real person known by God, and if these fetuses are not tossed directly into the pits of hell or into nothingness, based on this logic it only makes some kinda sense to me that a nation like China might receive a gold plaque from the Creator for sending the most souls to heaven with their enforced one-child policy. What really are the choices left to us from within an overcrowded land? You decide…

You who claim to know God, who make endless pages of laws and rules and sections and subsections full of neat and tidy, black and white regulations that instruct us how to get to heaven, casting a heavy burden upon the peoples' spirits—tell me, tell me that I might know, What are the precise and absolute measures of 'In Spirit and in Truth'? Did you care more for a mortal's soul cast into hell, with your prayers and fasting and tears, or more for the image of your church? You, with all your neatly arranged historical pages and books and letters and ledgers of the saved and of the damned, surely then you can draw for me the precise contours of the Great Spirit. *Did you really think that our Creator is ignorant of this all? Did you really think that those neat and tidy, black and white pages of baptisms and 'christianized' names, orderly numbers*

*of savages, pagans, heathens and 'civilized' that were 'saved',
and orderly certificates of church memberships, pages made
by ordinary mortals, would go unchallenged by the fire of our
Creator?*

Is it arrogance and blasphemy that comes from this
pen, you might ask? Tell me some of your own arrogance and
blasphemy that I might better understand what it is you ask of
me.

You see, perhaps it is not a title that we add to our
lives—politician, trapper, doctor, priest, pastor, carpenter,
waitress, scientist or clerk—that gets us an 'in' with our
Creator. Perhaps it is something much more profound and
simple than mere titles. Perhaps the Great Spirit of our Creator
works in such a way that confounds those who think themselves wise and of great importance. The world must tame
whom it can tame, to believe and espouse the game of which
we know not. Go ahead, laugh and ridicule the realm of spirit. Why then, the games of statues and tombstones and scattered ashes and funerals and remembrance days, if not to at
least in the smallest of measure seek some pittance of meaning to life, and a flicker against all odds of hope?

*"Oota nitayan Kichi Manitou, Kiwapamihin
nikiskeetheeteen"*—*"Here I am Great Spirit, You see me I
know." Who are You, Creator? What is it that You see that we
do not? How is it that You can see us for what we might really be? Is it true that You knew us before we left our mother's
womb, before we had any semblance of consciousness that we
might remember? Our DNA and cells that You created to hold
our body together to form a living, breathing human with the
capability to express emotion and reason and fear and hope.
Have we merely been fooled to think that we can think, to
think we are in control of all of our choices and actions? Is it
a cruel game that You play, or is it true that all along You
desired for us to reach out to You as a young child does to its
mother, that we might better know the base of true freedom?*

Sometimes I wonder if this is all a bunch of hogwash, or perhaps the Grace story is much bigger than I might think it to be—at least more profound. It only makes sense to me, God, that You know each of our funerals for what they truly are.

Seems to me, sometimes, that this funeral business of mortals takes a little planning after all.

"It seemed, and still seems to me, more reasonable to believe, not that God chose the Jews, but that the Jews were the first people that chose God, the first people in history to have done something truly revolutionary, and it was this choice that made them unique."

—Golda Meir, *My Life*

Pureblooded

I've never really had a whole lot of interest in my ancestry. Upon further reflection, I guess I did, except that I kinda backed all the way to Neanderthal man and apes and such. I suppose there must have been some kinda link for me between supposed Neanderthal man and the year 2008 A.D.

I write this story today to find out who I might be, without the knowing as to how this search might end, for it is not possible for a flawed mortal such as myself to write unflawlessly. I merely use my pen to arrange the pieces of patterns and codes that have come to me through such mediums as conversations, books, songs, movies, radio, ravens and owls. Caught up in the times and expression as all of us are; merely re-arranging the pieces of life's puzzle to see how sequences or mutations might fit.

The words flow easily, perhaps because they are merely simplistic, and it bewilders me sometimes how a mere pen moving about in my hand can help me to find out who I might be. Sometimes I am persuaded to ask this pen, "Who are you, and what is your name? You, who dabble with coded words—sometimes I can see You." Was it really possible, I wondered, that our Creator could actually speak to us in a dream or a vision or through a donkey? And then it struck me, was it possible that our Creator could actually speak to us through codes? Codes such as the words of ancient scriptures that were written by flawed mortals, words written in such a way that the coded arrangement showed that the writers of these words were grossly flawed and caught up in the times of their respective cultures—but through it all and in spite of it all there emerged a continuity of code patterns. Perhaps all along those codes were there, visible yet hidden. It is not given to youth to know all things, or to adults. At 47 years of age, I marvel at that which I was ignorant of only one year ago, and that which I was ignorant of the year before that, so that I do not and cannot trust myself so well. I see more that this pen, this mere pen, can so easily swing its power from humility to arrogance, from being a messenger of hope to promoting hatred. And the irony of it all is that this pen moves to how well I listen or how well I do not.

I was hoping that I could somehow acquire a genetic DNA blueprint of myself to prove that I am merely a mongrel, an assortment of various codes of humanity of brown and yellow and black and white. Within my recent ancestry, my father and mother, all I know is that I come from historically gentle and peace-loving peoples, which some might describe as Icelandic marauders and Germanic barbarians. My father, whose father came from Iceland as a young lad, met my mother in Germany around 1955 while he was in the Peace Corps. What liaisons both my mother's parents and my father's parents had in the past I know not, nor have I been inclined in any way as yet to search some of this past. All I know is that my mother and father fell in love and had five children, of which I am one. I know that my parents conceived me, but there was something within myself that intuitively led me to believe and to seek that I, humanity, am closely linked and known by our Creator. It was something that Gandhi knew well in seeking a just cause; for by seeking what we might believe to be a just cause, what we know intuitively to be right and pure, might resonate with the people. It is as if it is something that our Creator has instilled in each one of us that we cannot always see because of our own folly that blurs our vision, a code within that tells us we are all created equal.

And I thought it strange to think about humanity's tangled web of which we are all a part, to look back in my life to how I reacted, then and now, to my perceptions of life. For most of my years I would answer when asked that I was Icelandic; after all, wasn't that what people were wondering about, the origin of the name Bjornson? I was born in 1960 and, strangely, even as youngsters we somehow have an intuition, perhaps instilled by such things as conversations and jokes and the history that we are each taught within our communities of our nations, as to what we are willing to disclose and what we might try to hide. It was a sub-conscious hiding of our past, but why? My mother was from Germany, and the association with Hitler and the terrible wars and the Holocaust was somehow a part of my past that I did not want anyone to know. My mother was only a teenager at the end of World War II, so it did not make any sense to think that she was the main instigator for those tragic days. But word-associations are something that we, humanity, are sometimes quick to point a finger at with all the power and authority of our 'highly-enlightened' wisdom. We sometimes dare to think to be a German is to be all Germans, to be an Indian is to be all Indians, to be a Christian is to be all Christians, to be a Muslim is to be all Muslims, to be a Liberal is to be all Liberals. The associations are sometimes still with us. It is a knowing somehow, whether we admit it or not, that history is not so easily forgotten—at least by those who remember it. So it seemed natural at the time to keep quiet about that part of me. But when mothers of sons and daughters pass on, sometimes there is a link that is, for whatever reason, opened up and rejoined, so that now I can say with full confidence: I am my mother's son.

During the time of my mother's funeral, I was visiting at my father's apartment with various relatives who I really did not know very well. It was only natural for me to wonder who the fellow with the darker skin was that sat not far away. It was explained by my aunt that her father, my dad's father, had married a full-blooded Indian woman from North Dakota. (My father later said that she was only a half-breed, whatever the case may be.) My grandfather and his first wife had two children before she died, two aunts of mine whom I had met only a couple of times who had both passed on, and this darker skinned man was a son of one of them. Who was this Indian woman, and from what tribe was she, what language did she speak? Why was it that I was told this at my mother's funeral and not before? When my aunt told me of this piece of family history, my curiosity piqued greatly. She, in the next sentence, tried to reassure me that my grandfather's second wife, who was my grandmother, was a full-blooded Icelander, supposedly to reassure me. For a moment I had been excited that perhaps I was fortunate and blessed enough to have some Indian blood in me, but then, if that were true, why was this kept so secret? My natural inclination was to find out where a fellow could be tested for the codes of DNA, if it could be tested in a manner that might show the percentage of different races of people I was descended from, and how much this might cost. You see, it really did not matter in any way whatsoever to me, for I knew that I could say with full confidence that I am my father's son.

I merely wanted to prove, for myself and for humanity, that I am a mongrel and loved by my Creator. I merely wanted to prove scientifically that, in layman's terms, there is no such thing as a pureblooded or a full-blooded people; our blood merely proves that we are of the human kind. I wanted to prove that when humanity found the code that could show us each individually the genetic percentage of our background and skin colour, the differences were so minute. That if we were to determine on a scale who was black enough to be black, who was brown enough to be brown, or who was white enough to be white, we are all of us a mixture of a little bit of this and that—proving that we are all mongrels but still loved by our Creator.

Webster's defines colour as "a sensation rather than a property of a thing". If this be true, then, tragically, humanity has often been caught up in a game of sensationalism. And if some mortals were to dabble in the game, the dangerous game, as to decide where on the chart of life one is black enough to be black, one is brown enough to be brown, or one is white enough to be white, who is it that would decide this magical colour code? For is not what is 'pure' and 'full' a complete numerical and unbroken code, an unaltered sequence? Is not one-trillionth of an altered sequence a broken or changed or mutated code? What mortal then can boast of being full and pure, except to say that we are fully and purely human? Identical twins could boast of a similar sequence of DNA, yet they still carry a slightly altered sequence from the rest of the world's identical twins, and each identical twin carries still different codes from each other such as differing fingerprints and personalities.

If we believe that humans evolved over millions of year—such as the colours of our skin adapting to various environments over long periods of time—does this not prove that we are all of us a little bit of this and a little bit of that? For in this game does not even one-trillionth of an altered or mutated code prove we are all of us mongrels? And even if we might believe in Creation that black was made black and white was made white and brown was made brown, throughout the millennia of our existence and interaction with each other does this not also prove the extreme probability that we are all of us a little bit of this and a little bit of that? For in this game does not even one-trillionth of an altered or mutated code prove we are all of us mongrels?

Humanity had it tragically wrong all along when we played the dangerous game of which skin colour is more holy or more caring or more wise or more savage. Humanity had it wrong when we thought that skin colour could tell us who is superior and who is inferior. The codes were present all along, so blatantly obvious yet we could not see because we were distracted by mere sensation. The ways of how we address our heritage and background and skin colour are as varied as the shades of all that we are or believe we are; as varied as to who might be the subjugated and who the rulers might be in a particular nation at a particular time-frame of history; as varied as politics and tyrants; as varied as pride or fear.

Should not the words be just when written so boldly, intuitive truths written in such a way that they might resonate with the people, encoded all along in the recesses of our conscience? I write these words that I might be cursed by all colours of people, and I write these same words that all colours of people might know a piece of the trail of hope.

I can only write as to what I boldly know for sure, as sure as the dawn brings a new day: I am my mother's and father's son. I was loved by my parents. I am a mongrel. I am a pureblooded and a full-blooded human being. I am fully known and understood to the exact sequence of codes that I might be, as we all are. And for whatever mysterious reason and grace, I am loved by my Creator.

Yet Another
Letter to Revenue Canada

April 3, 2008

Revenue Canada
Winnipeg, MB

Hello the camp, Revenue Canada, it's only me again,

 Name—Ingi
 Skin colour and DNA profile—as of today I'm kinda
whitish skin, except from my neck up which is much browned
from a sensuous affair of kissing the spring sun. My blood
type is one where the code-mutation has been altered at least
one-trillionth throughout the course of humanity's beginnings,
which of course makes me a mongrel but a pureblooded and
full-blooded human being.

Academic education—grade 10 with a C- average. I always took the stupid math course so I could finish early and draw my little log cabin with smoke rising up the chimney as the snow fell amid spruce trees and a pile of firewood with an axe embedded in a stump.

Dreams—one fine wife with a couple of fine children and dogs who would fly out to the trapline with me each year and stay in the little log cabin.

Reality of life—one fine wife with a couple of fine children and dogs who have flown out to the trapline with me each year, that is until my boys got grown up.

Retirement plan—one fine wife with a couple of children to visit with every so often, and a good dog who would walk my secret trail with me and come on canoe trips and a wife who would still continue to fly out to the trapline with me each autumn, although she says she will only come with me in the deep bush until she is 82 years old. Oh yes, and a little log cabin…

Political preference—the politician who knows a piece of humility.

Favorite drink—the one laced with good conversation.

Religious belief—I believe in some kinda Creator.

More specific religious belief—I am a scoundrel who knows, in part, the trail of Grace.

Favorite sermon—I have heard many fine sermons, but none so fine as the bubbling brook.

Nation of residence—*Kanata* (Canada), a nation as we know it, so far, founded by the First Nations people inhabiting these lands for thousands of years, culminating into supposedly 55 distinct Nation-cultures at the time of the European contact some 400 years ago (although the Beothuks of Newfoundland were all "successfully" exterminated with the last known survivor dying in 1829). About 400 years ago the French and the British came over and had their squabbles, which kinda culminated in a political decision on the Plains of

Abraham in 1759 with the official defeat of the French; the politics and numbers and the decisions of the times reflecting who might be a savage or civilized human being, which has us as a nation to this day trying to maintain a semblance of a unified country. And then came the hordes of various other immigrants once the plains were surveyed and the railroads built and the buffalo killed off: Germans, Russians, Irish, Scottish—you name it, they came. This of course merely proves that we have an on-going Canadian Accord. All nations have their challenges, and I feel privileged and pleased to live on Canadian soil.

Credentials—one who dabbles in wine, a hermit, a B.S er, a loser-writer (from what I've been told), and my wife says I'm special.

I just found out today from Cindy that the interpretation of the registered letter dated March 27, 2008, is that we are being audited on our 2005 fiscal year. It was not my first choice of what to work on today since we just went through a three-year-long audit. I can't quite figure out why we are being audited again, but I gather it has something to do with the folks from our accountant's office trying to carry over some losses to the years we were just audited on, namely 2003 and '04. I asked my fine wife what this was all about, and she said the accountant's office had mentioned this to her and she had responded, "That's fine."

Now, one can suppose that this might have pressed certain buttons at Revenue Canada by trying to legitimately recoup penalties from our recent audit. Even a man such as I can figure this out with my academic weight. But I suppose our accountant's motive was genuine, and is it not an honourable thing to seek a semblance of genuinity? Cindy always does the town business since I am somewhat challenged in certain aspects of business.

Some people have told me that I ought to get out more and see people, and I suppose it sure don't hurt to try to maintain some semblance of social skills. Of course, when I look at some of the pale faces of those who have told me to get out more, I wondered when was the last time they had looked in a mirror to see their own pale reflection from sitting in front of a computer screen all day, or their stress lines from rushing along on a full calendar that they themselves choose to follow—without taking the time to kiss the spring sun and listen for the first eagle, the first crow, or the first drip.

I have not, within the tyranny of my own little mind, officially closed our long audit, since we have still not received the substantial refund cheque that we were notified of prior to Christmas. (Yes, we have the letter from the Appeals Department.) Seems to me it is kinda taking a long time to come. I do not know if we will receive added interest and penalties from Revenue Canada like you of Revenue Canada are quick to add on to the average citizen being audited. Though, of course, I do not seek interest and penalties. Cindy informs me that the monies are slow in coming from Revenue Canada because our accountant took a while to do the paperwork of finishing our fiscal year end, or something like that. I do know that if payment was required from the citizen, Revenue Canada would frown on having to wait many months. But I suppose that it is normal to have varying standards in life.

Let it be noted that the financial costs are becoming quite substantial for a little enterprise such as ours, an additional $950 just from the accountant's office because of helping with our long audit, with another bill to come next year. Although I kinda think that our accountant is going easy on us, and for that I am grateful. And now, with another audit immediately starting, our costs will again accrue. One might suppose that audits can be good economic circles for accounting businesses, since this gives them more work to do and results in a higher bill for their clients. On the other hand, accountants might then have to deal with irate clients or a measure of intimidation or annoyance from having Revenue Canada on their backs. I suppose, then, that by and large accountants and their clients would probably prefer to not have Revenue Canada visiting them—at least not too often. It is also reasonable to suggest that even Revenue Canada would not like to have certain people visiting them too often—knowing the secret combination to enter through their front door. And so we all of us are a part of the circle of accountability. There are some advantages though from having back-to-back audits: we are now on a familiar first-name basis—Catherine, Cindy, John, Bob, Tina, Nazir, Linda, and, of course, Ingi. (Though of course we'll have to take out names in this letter when it is printed in book form, for privacy's sake.)

You will know, Revenue Canada, by the codes of this letter that it is not written just for you. And I too know that this new audit is not just for Cindy and me. Image will seek to play the winning card. I will not seek to defend my fine name, because it is not such a fine name, but it is enough that my parents and wife and two sons and two dogs have loved me. Whatever charges you may find to degrade my little name, I will help you to degrade it even more. And so, I seek the popular vote.

A stranger said to me the other day that Revenue Canada does not have a sense of humour. I do not know what experience that fellow has had with you or with life to say such a thing, but it is my firm belief that all institutions consist of mere and real human beings. And that is why I know in my heart that the real people who work for Revenue Canada do in fact have a sense of humour, for the traits of humanity are inherent and not defined or contained by mere job titles, although it is indeed true that certain institutions or individuals will put much emphasis on the games of image.

It is my delusion and flaw, if it is a flaw, to try to treat people as equal. And as I had written before, you of Revenue Canada are welcome in my camp anytime, and I shall put on a pot of coffee or tea. Dang it all though, the financial costs are starting to climb—perhaps (and this is a shameful promotion on my part within the realm of capitalism and commerce) you folks of Revenue Canada might choose to stay in our camp and rent a cabin of ours when you are in the area to audit someone, as this could help to offset the costs of our audits and the challenges with tourism, what with high gas prices and a weak U.S. dollar. You may come here with a semblance of genuinity and honesty, as social or more private beings, any of which I will respect, or you may come dressed up secretively and undercover. It don't matter to me, besides, we know not who plays the game of whom sometimes. And we might all sit around the campfire with a hot coffee or cool beer or cup of wine while the loons sing, and talk of life, and there shall be no bitterness from me whatsoever, but only a mutual appreciation of the bounty and wonder of the land. And we might talk of our search for a sense of continuity in life, as various friends and loved ones and acquaintances pass on and sometimes leave us uprooted for a while, and in spite of the frailty of being human, we still might find pieces of continuity to help sustain us through troubled times.

It is my pathetic makeup of being human in seeking to deal with a tangible face of humanity regardless of whatever name an institution might have, and I am gladdened by the familiarity of a now first-name basis. If Cindy and I are to go through yet another audit immediately following the previous long one, then you of Revenue Canada will know that Ingi was a part of it. If I were to somehow sum up the previous audit for my fellow citizens, I would say: "If it is not in your heart to follow a pattern of corruption with the government of which we are all a part, do not be intimidated or lose any sleep. If you are being audited by Revenue Canada and have something to hide—watch out, be intimidated, and lose sleep, because the auditors do their job very well."

Granted, you will undoubtedly find a few mistakes within our 2005 paper trails, as within any fiscal year of any individual or corporate structure. I say this knowingly and with full confidence within the code patterns of humanity: that it is only human to err. Personally, I make mistakes about every other day, although Cindy says it is more like a couple times a day, and I'm inclined to agree with her. But again, what you will not find is a patterned trail of corruption, because it is not there, and that is why I will lose no sleep or be intimidated. Nor will Revenue Canada by this next audit intimidate Cindy and I into changing our declaration habits, we will continue to by and large declare our earnings.

Again, I say this knowingly that I am a thief, a habitual breaker of laws, and a fake. If one has stolen five dollars (or one pound of wild rice, or that ten dollar tip that I did not declare and used to take Cindy out for a cup of coffee) one is a thief. If one habitually drives one kilometer over the speed limit, one is a habitual breaker of the law. (No surprise, I'm guilty of this as well. Even my young son, who became sworn in as an RCMP in December '07, says that he drives 106 in a 100 kph speed zone in his cruiser car. He is only 19 years old and probably this acceptable speed would have been suggested to him from other members in the force. Okay, I admit it, I often drive 108 in a 100 kph zone—of course, only 101 kph is breaking the law.) And I am a fake in many ways because I refuse to listen closer to the cries of the oppressed, or listen closer to the inner voice that beckons to us all. For these practical and legitimate reasons, we are admonished not to sweat the small stuff. For reasons such as these, I seek the song of the quandary, to perhaps better know what it is to be human. The greater the perceived image, the greater it must do to uphold itself—Who are you and what is your name?

Please take note of another extent of my thievery: we collect roughly $85 worth of beer cans each season from our summer guests. Monies that I suppose should be declared to Revenue Canada, but which we cash in and Cindy then treats us to a twice-yearly treat of Kentucky Fried Chicken from town. I don't really have much say on the matter, but we sure enjoy the treat. I also gather along the local road perhaps an additional $25 of beer cans that I do not declare, but those beer cans are not a direct earning for our business, merely the mess of various locals or other travelers in the area.

Also note that we have not used legitimate write-offs for the past several years, such as food for our two dogs that are very directly involved in guarding our camp from the almost daily visits of bears during the early summer. You see, because of our low earnings since roughly the year 2000, we have not had the need to write off all of our legitimate expenses.

Cindy had explained to me that because of a couple of little mistakes from the audit division in the previous audit, certain portions were thrown out. In my own little mind there is no honour in this, for all of us mortals make mistakes in life. There is the story I heard of a professor who said to a new group of those starting a law degree: "To those of you here who come to seek justice, you might as well walk out now. We are here to deal with the letter and technicality of the law." To counter that, a naïve hermit might say: "Seek justice, for it is an honourable calling. What is it to you if some have been bribed by six-digit salaries, where the laws have merely become a game of chess, moved about in such a way to let someone off because of a technicality? Where is the honour in this?"

I just wanted to write to you, our previous auditor or whoever works on our file, to encourage you to seek justice. And I hereby overrule, via this letter which must be kept in your file, any portion of the Audit Appeals Division or our accountant who might seek to let us off of a charge because of a mere technicality, a mere mistake by an auditor, because it is only human to err. Why should someone who has done his or her job well be overruled because of a technical mistake? Have the courts sometimes turned into a Pharisee-like game of petty squabbles where the squabbles of technicality take precedence over justice, where greater wealth can hire greater lawyers to greaten the chance of finding a little technicality? I must choose the honourable course. Granted, overruling (in my little mind) any future appeals of this new audit because of a technicality might be setting a dangerous precedent, why, that could uproot the structure of the courts as we might perceive it to be—justice taking precedent over technicalities, may it never be! To believe, or to delude oneself into believing, in a just cause as the mighty river rushes against one can be daunting and bewildering at times. And sometimes the man thinks to himself at night when he awakens: *What on earth does this have to do with me? I am only a scoundrel. What do You want with me?* How many cries will it take to convince one of a just cause? Will the voices of 20,000 ghosts be enough? John Newton thought so.

Yes, some have told me I am a naïve man, and so sometimes one must play the game of which one is accused. "Don't write another letter" some might say, but I suppose that those same folks might have had something to hide by saying that, and I suppose they were too naïve to know that there are real, live, flesh-and-blood people comprised of spirit behind any and every institution of our nation or other nations; real people with flaws and hopes and dreams and biases and struggles and strengths. And so I seek a tangible link within humanity. We all of us sift through the codes and patterns of life to make some kinda sense, even as the pen moves in my hand it prods me to sift through the codes. Perhaps, then, the arranging of words which are merely codes helps me to make pieces of sense as I write to you, and the pen might give me more boldness and discernment to make certain decisions that I otherwise might not have made. The greater that image must do to uphold itself, the greater the freedom that comes from within me, and it only makes sense. Within the games of image I will lose, but I will be free. You have my full blessing on this new audit.

Thank you for the correspondence.

To breathe in is to know I am alive,
to breathe out is to know I have lived.

Ingi

cc accountant's office
cc a good friend
cc previous, retired accountant
cc another good friend

"For twelve years I was taught to love my neighbour—especially if he was white—but to hate myself. I was made to feel untrustworthy, inferior, incapable, and immoral. The barbarian in me, I was told, had to be destroyed if I was to be saved. I was taught to feel nothing but shame for my 'pagan savage' ancestors... When I had been stripped of all pride, self-respect, and self-confidence, I was told to make something of myself..."

—Jane Willis, Cree woman from the James Bay region of Quebec, describing her residential school experience of the 1940s and '50s. *The Dispossessed*

"When your nation lives a lie, God cannot allow that lie to prevail. Because your cause is just, it will prevail. One day, you will be free in the way you want to be free."

—1990, Archbishop Desmond Tutu, speaking to the Ogibway people of the Osnaburgh reserve. *The Dispossessed*

For Whom Has Sang
a Just Cause

February 20, 2008

Hello the camp, to my past, present or future fellow citizens of Canada and our past, present or future government of which we all are a part,

It may sit for a little while yet, but it will come, even the oracles of time have known this. In this letter I have sought the song of the quandary, wherein the song might perhaps lead us to consider turning the page. This letter will slip through the weak spots of an 'efficient society', because the codes are designed that way, and it only makes sense that everything in life has a code.

It has been written 'ask and you shall receive,' although it only makes some kinda sense that we cannot have everything that we ask for, but the chance of receiving is lessened if we do not ask. What personal gain is it to me to ask? None. It is not for me, but it extends from within me, with the hope that perhaps enough of my fellow citizens might see the need of it. Perhaps even a 20% portion of the people of Canada might be enough to help persuade our government to consider it, perhaps even as little as 10%, perhaps this one letter? But it is not just the sounds of this little letter, for this letter is merely a reflection and weight of the voices past and present and yet to come. It is not yet historically proven which noise can have a more profound impact: the crack of a cannon or the first call of the young loon, the well-trod trail of the masses or the faint trail of the wanderer.

Is it not fair to ask for forgiveness if one has done wrong? It is what I have been taught by my parents, teachers, Sunday school, my wife—unless of course they were all just liars. I was generally taught that it is a good thing to say sorry if I have done wrong. Yet within the context of the subject of this letter, what wrong have I done? I have refused to look at another view of history for too many years, I have said cruel jokes about a dispossessed people, and I have laughed along with others when they have made cruel jokes about a dispossessed people, these jokes being told both outside and inside of a church. It is my complete and utter folly if I now believe with all my heart that my Creator has made us all equal—brown, yellow, black and white. And if I now believe this to be true, then it challenges certain things that I have been earlier taught. It now causes me to react differently to words from the early 1700s such as: *One colonizing Puritan wrote: "The good hand of God favoured our beginnings in sweeping away the multitudes of the Natives by the small pox."*

Is it true, God, that You favoured the recent immigrants more so than the Indian peoples by allowing various diseases to run rampant amongst them? Is it true, then, that You favoured the white man so much that we could build all kinds of monstrous machinery and technology that could tear apart mountains and spew all kinds of smoke and gases and chemicals that could help foul the air that we breathe and the water that we drink—all in the name of progress?

It is not so easy to discuss certain things with the masses of humanity, and so I merely seek the movements of my pen, with the knowing that my Creator can see me within and without for all that I might be. I know within my heart that the movement of my pen is not designed for a mass market. Shall my pen then merely rise to the terror of its own tyranny—following the patterned course of all of human nature that has been and has yet to come? Alas, I am indeed caught up in the box. It is my utter folly, and yet my pen sometimes moves with ease to something beyond myself—that is for portions of humanity to try to decide, whether now or after the passing of many years. Like a new day that has begun with calm winds, it is for some things not to be known which way they might blow until the sun has again set.

Many times I have heard it said, "I had nothing to do with that. That was during my forefathers' time." That statement, of course, proves that we are indeed linked with history; even biblical writings substantiate this ideal by such writings as the sin of our forefathers visiting us in the first, second and third generations to come. *Jesus replied, "Woe to you, because you build tombs for the prophets, and it was your forefathers who killed them. So you testify that you approve of what your forefathers did; they killed the prophets, and you build their tombs."* How can I/we/whoever might read into the words of this Jesus, how can we now say that history is in no way tied to our present? Our very words—our body-language—gives us away. It is true that we did not build tombs for the dispossessed of our nation; we merely plowed, built, flooded over or tried to build a golf course over their graves.

Did you not see it, there, right before our eyes—the story? It rests there plainly amid all of the chaos and clutter

and tangled web of all that we are, not to be seen until we ourselves are ready to look. And it only makes sense that something cannot be better seen until we are better ready to look.

I have heard it said from some that an apology from
the government could not come because it might prove too
expensive. But it has always been true that an apology is not
for free—for then it fully admits that the asker of it has done
wrong, and to admit to being wrong requires a sometimes rare
humility which might ruffle our pride for awhile. And if the
concern in this case is that an apology might be perceived to
be too financially costly, does this not merely prove in itself
that the wrong that was done was of enormous proportions, of
such a magnitude that portions of our history books might
have to be rewritten, that portions of the government and the
church might have to re-tally the code, that the dictionary
might have to redefine what is civilized and what is savage,
that our Creator does indeed see brown and yellow and black
and white as equal?

Has there not been a remnant of honourable people
from within the different tribes or nations of our world? A
remnant who are not bribed so easily, those who intuitively
knew that they could not be easily bribed by money, with the
knowing that money cannot and never could buy the spirit to
lift one's head in pride—to know one is of equal status before
our Creator and of the peoples all about them. A knowing
within of the profound power of an apology, because the apology would acknowledge the wrongs done and lay a foundation
from which to rebuild, and the patterns and codes might begin
to make more sense to the youth who, like all of us, desperately need to make some kinda sense in a sometimes chaotic
world.

Did you not see the slap in the face for the dispossessed when the Japanese received an official apology for
their internment on Canadian soil, and the apology to the
Chinese for their head-tax, and the motives behind the Meech

Lake accord that tried to base itself on two founding peoples? If the apology for the dispossessed was to be measured by giving monies per those individuals affected by the great upheaval, and giving the traditional lands back, our nation would go broke. That is the enormity of what happened to the dispossessed peoples: Indians, Métis, those people 'tainted' with the savage and sub-standard Indian blood, scattered on and off their reservations. It is our legacy, our dark history, the story was always open for all to see, but it is meant for stories to be kept secret until we are ready to turn the page, and it only makes sense. A truly proud people cannot be bought, nor can a true and honourable apology be bribed with money, yet is not an apology a profound foundation from which to start?

It is a given that not all citizens would embrace a public apology from the government, perhaps even the majority would not. Nor could the majority of the dispossessed be expected to accept an apology from our Canadian government without some form of compensation, but there is a remnant who would recognize the apology as a profound thing—a foundation to build a cornerstone of understanding. Waves of immigrants keep washing ashore from all over the world, filling, in part, the vacuum of the labour shortage of our demographic challenge in our nation at this time of history. A recent census by our government now shows roughly 41% people of Asian descent, with only 37% people of European descent. The white man is now a minority again on Canadian soil. It is given to all stories and tales to have patterns and codes, memory-associations relative to the experience. Those people of the dispossessed have their valid association-memories that will not be washed away, no more than each and every other person from Canada or any other recent immigrant that has moved here have their own association-memories; consumed by the trials and trails of their/our own individual and cultural lives—yet even with all the multitudes of immigrants both old and new within the last 400 years it is not enough to crush the voice of the dispossessed. The voices of the dispossessed will grow louder in the coming years, the drumbeat will not be kept quiet, and various levels of governments will continue to come together to discuss the how's and the why's and how they, we, might try to work together to help overcome a dark piece of our history. It never was possible to bribe spirit in this world; the pure spirit that our living Creator has given to us all, residing, resting, pulsing within each and every one of us, seeking to make our soul free; the pure spirit that desired to consume us with all the goodness of our Creator—but it would be suppressed for short times and lengthy times, after all, it never was an easy road to be human. Perhaps, then, a piece of the code of goodness could reside in something as profoundly simple as a national apology.

I have heard it said by some non-Indians, after they had talked with an Indian, "They are just regular people like us." And I suspect that some of the Indian peoples have made more than a few jokes and chuckles about the non-Indians in regard to statements like this. It is true, we are all people, and always were; our blood is the blood of the people because that is the way our Creator has made it to be. Some have said, "Why should we keep giving money and houses to the Indians? What more do they want? Don't they know that pride and keeping one's head up cannot be bought with money?" But the story that was always there to see merely by turning the page would rarely be turned. It was not the Indians who set up the reservations or the houses often packed with 12 or more people or the welfare cheques, it was we, the non-Indian government, trying to ease our conscience somewhat in the taking over of their lands and lives and religions. It is a part of our Canadian legacy, and we will reap what we have sown.

I have asked many, and I will continue to ask. I asked an Indian woman recently about why sometimes Indians (First Nations people) will not make direct eye contact with others; is it more to do with the historical cultures of their peoples or more to do with the great upheavals the Indians have gone through? Each person answers in their own way, but her answer was, "Because we had been knocked and beaten down over and over for so many centuries and treated like second-class people for so long that we walk about with our heads lowered. But we will rise again. And we are beginning to rise and unify more." I asked her if it was still possible to build little bridges between Indians and non-Indians, and she answered, "Yes." And I asked her if a public apology from the government might be profound enough to mean something, anything, at least to a portion of the Indian people, because ultimately does not a national apology in its very least acknowledge the past, or at least portions of it? She answered that "Yes, it would mean something." I said to her that in my heart I believed that an apology might come sooner rather than later. And then I asked if she thought that the Indian people would receive an apology, to which she answered, "Probably not." And she went on to tell me that "The First Nations people would rise again and their voice would not be suppressed."

That same day I had asked a non-Indian if a national apology to the First Nations could perhaps be a tiny cornerstone of understanding, to which he said rather irately with a condescending body language, "Who knows! Do you know?! The answer is like that song that says: The answer is blowing in the wind!" It was not until the next day as I snowshoed on my secret trail with my dogs that, as I thought about what he had said, I realized that he was right, and by saying what he had said had merely proved that the answer, or at least portions and pieces of the answer, was indeed blowing in the wind. It was not vanity after all. We, all of us, swim about in an ocean of life-giving air—sometimes calm and sometimes windy. We have all of us lived and breathed the same air of this planet, so it only made some kinda sense that pieces and portions of understanding might be had by turning the page of a windy day.

I knew from within my heart that the First Nations would rise again and that their voice would grow, because even the oracles of time have known this. But it is not for me to force anyone to turn the page that might help unravel some of the mysteries of life, the page will turn all by itself because that has always been the nature of history's heart beat. The unturned pages were not mysteries all along, they were only more of a mystery to those of us who had not taken the time to turn the page. But I suppose that life is kinda like that. Perhaps, though, I thought from within a thought that I did not even know where the original thought came, the timing of the turning of the page could have a variable impact as to the meaning and sincerity of a national apology and to the integral strength of the bridges that we will one day look back on.

If the apology came later rather than sooner, at a time when the First Nations people grew to such numbers that greater numbers of frustrated youth would be harder and harder to handle, an apology might tend to be seen more as a political 'need' or of a greater 'coercion' rather than a more genuine heart meaning. No one ever said that saying sorry is easy, it never has been, but the consequences of not apologizing at all will make things harder, and it only makes sense. There is room to learn understanding from both sides of the fence, from both sides—variable sides—of the past, a tangled web of whom we all are that swim about in the same ocean of air. Each culture, each language, holds a piece of the puzzle and code of humanity, because that is the way our Creator has made it to be, and we have all of us been given a sometimes terrible and wonderful freedom.

We who bide the time and consciously or sub-consciously pass on the days of history onto another generation, we are now the forefathers and foremothers. What will be said of us? For those who might preach assimilation at all cost and might shake their heads in self-righteous frustration: turn the page and seek to read into it, seek discernment and understanding and you may hear the song of the quandary. Not all Indians nor non-Indians will accept an apology on behalf of our government. We cannot, and never can, turn back the clock, it is the way our Creator has made it to be for mortals. Spirit cannot, and never could be bribed. An apology will not, and never could, immediately fix all of the repercussions of the wrong done. But in itself it is a powerful and profound cornerstone that would shake up some of the writings of history and some of the tallies of the church. Perhaps a national apology to the Indians, status and non-status, the Métis, for all those carrying the 'tainted blood' and all those entwined, would help to build a bridge of understanding.

If apologies can be weighed by the amount of a peoples' blood, expropriation of lands, herded onto reservations, forbidden to speak their own languages by various governments and churches of the land, children taken from their homes and forced into residential schools, not able to vote until 1960 on their reservations, and treated as second-class citizens, there are no apologies combined more weightier than all of this within the last 150 years on Canadian soil. If apologies can be weighed by economics, as to which peoples might tend to work 60 hours or more per week and seek to fatten a bank account or live by the standards of ever-consuming, finding meaning in a crowded shopping mall where happiness might be based on ever-purchasing, taking a grind at the wheel of the incentives of capitalism where there is little time left to listen for the faint song of the chickadee, where the lands are ever being taken over by concrete and steel so that there is less and less room for the wolf and the grizzly bear to travel, then there is little need to apologize to the First Nations peoples of Canada; so sang, the song of the quandary. Will the wealth of our nation be based on gold bars or a clean land? Will our ultimate worth as individuals be based on the pursuit of gold or the pursuit of a clean land? Surely, we can all of us learn a little bit from another culture.

Canada, like a beating heart you have boldly told me that history is indeed tied to the past by your, our, recent apologies to the Japanese for their internment, and to the Chinese for their head-tax, and how the Meech Lake accord was destroyed by a single eagle feather. From all the stories of parents or teachers or any perceived mentor who has said that a pattern of a loving and stable home might tend to give a child more stability in life, from all the stories of psychiatrists and psychologists who might seek to read into the human heart and mind and all that we might be, and who might say that a broken and dysfunctional and uprooted home could tend to leave a greater pattern of broken and unstable and uprooted children in their wake, will you now tell me that history is not linked to our past? From the time of 1885 that Louis Riel—who was hanged for treason and now in the province of Manitoba of 2008 we have an official Louis Riel Day—do you not see the code, the code that boldly tells us that history is most often written and favoured by the conquerors, the code that boldly tells us that recorded history does not necessarily beget truth? Tell me it is all a lie and a hoax, a continual scam, and I shall put my pen down and rid myself of these thoughts that will not leave me alone.

You whom breathe the winds of time, can you not feel it, sense it, discern it—the faint breeze of history's heart beat? Did we not seek the code of an integral bridge of understanding by apologizing to the Japanese and the Chinese, to help ease the 'grave injustice' of our past? As honourable and good as it may be, you, we, as a nation, cannot, must not, make any more historical apologies to any peoples without first making a national apology to those of Indian blood. Do you not see the slap in the face for the dispossessed? Do you not hear their cry? No peoples of our nation within the last 150 years have gone through greater upheavals, combined, than the great upheaval of the Indian peoples. For whom has sang the song of a just cause?

Perhaps it will not be a popular vote—a risk for the one who leads our nation, but whomever makes this decision will be remembered well in history. But beyond all this, in the day that all of the history books and the tallies of the church and all of the tangled web of humanity that must pass through the fire of our Creator, my heart tells me that our Creator will look favorably at anyone, for little reasons or great reasons, who might from a genuine heart seek a cornerstone of understanding by a little apology.

When the apology does come it will not bring a quick and radical change of understanding for Indians or non-Indians, but to those of the Indian blood who might know it for what it really might be, an acknowledgement of our dark history, their spirit that the Creator has given them will be much stirred and they will hold their heads a little higher. And a tiny cornerstone of understanding might be set in place.

Monies will continue to be given to the Indian peoples, more youth will start to leave the reservations and we will desperately try to encourage them to 'come aboard' and fill the jobs of our labour vacuum; the patterns and codes were set in their place. I will not write to seek pieces of motives and backroom deals and such, but I will tell you that the chickadee had landed beside me and sang its song.

The patterns of what will come will come anyways, because that is the nature of history's heart beat of which we are all a part. Did you not walk ahead and look back? The recent huge payouts for those of the residential schools—some remember it as a good experience but most do not—the enormities of the monies boldly tells me, us, that something enormous happened. Do not seek to stir the peoples and divide the camp of a just cause, because a just cause will carry through. Do not attempt to bribe a pure spirit because a pure spirit cannot be bribed. Like a new day that has begun with calm winds, it is for some things not to be known which way they might blow until the sun has set. To have looked back with a national apology in the history books will be a better course, this is what my heart pleads to tell you. I have become more aware of the price-tag of my life for penning words, are you more aware of yours? Who will attempt to bribe spirit? So sang, the song of the quandary.

I, within my own cubicle and lack of understanding, seek and ask not for a bribed apology from our nation, not one with a price tag, but a simple and freely given one that might be, and ultimately is, vastly more profound than a purchased apology, that the 'tainted Indian blood' scam and all that it led to would be seen for what it truly is—an insult to science and humanity and to our Creator—and that the Indian peoples could hold their heads high, and that little bridges could be built. So sang, the song of the quandary. Whom will be so bold?

I cast my vote in favour.

Sincerely,
Ingi G. Bjornson

cc Queen Elizabeth, or the Queen or King to come
cc The Prime Minister of Canada, Stephen Harper, or the one to come
cc The peoples of Canada, or the peoples to come
cc MP Tina Keeper, or the MP to come
cc MLA Gerard Jennissen, or the MLA to come
cc John Leclair
cc Bob Hay
cc Jon Donald
cc Irvin Head

A profound thing happened on June 11th, 2008, that caused the nation of Canada to stop for a moment. Our Prime Minister, Stephen Harper, addressed the nation with a public apology to those of Inuit or Indian or Métis blood—all those that were forced into the residential schools and all the evil that it led to. No mortal must be let loose with the tyranny of power, be it a politician, priest, teacher, plumber, hunter, hairdresser, or writer.

In my heart I believe that Stephen Harper spoke from a genuine tongue. To those who might know the history of our nation, it is as Grand Chief Phil Fontaine spoke: "the impossible happened." Another profound thing happened: the leaders of the N.D.P. and the Liberals also spoke up with an apology to the First Nations—the House of Commons was united in solemn agreement that caused the nation of Canada to stop for a moment. An inherently just cause was enough to unite all of Canada's political parties for a sacred moment, because it is the inherent nature of a just cause to convict the spirit of humanity. Who will attempt to bribe spirit?

About 2:00 a.m. on June 11, I awoke from a vivid dream. In it I saw what looked like a well-dressed man, wearing a suit and tie, walking quickly past me, and I recognized it. I started to follow, when it sensed me and started running away. It leaped over a railing, diving head first to the edge of a concrete floor and a wall twenty feet below, and then simply disappeared into it. For some reason I recognized the code

id began to taunt it, and the greater I taunted the greater this
heinous creature began to emerge. And as I loudly taunted, it
tried to reach up and grab me; when I became quiet and it
could no longer see me, it slowly vanished. It was not until I
started to write about this creature that the dream began to
make sense, that heinous creature was powerless to stop a just
cause.

The codes of the song of the quandary were always
present, the secret was never a secret. It was merely by turning the page that we might catch a glimpse of it, and the
pleadings within my heart tell me that the better course was
chosen. Thank you, Prime Minister Stephen Harper, and to the
leaders of Canada's other political parties, and all those who
could not run away from a just cause; you have chosen well.

It is the inherent nature of humanity to reap what we
have sown, both as individuals and as a nation. We will still
have our challenges and a desperate need to bridge the past,
but the better course has been chosen, and a cornerstone of
understanding has been set in place. Portions of the 'official'
history books and the 'official' tallies of the church can now,
justly, be challenged, because a piece of our dark history has
been acknowledged. There will be more pressures now to deal
with such things as land claims issues. The money pot will
shrink with the coming demographic challenges for a time,
but the dispossesed of our nation will now have more reason
to hold their heads high.

What happened on June 11th, 2008, was the culmina-
tion of many voices, but none more so than the voices of the
dispossesed peoples who had everything taken from them; and
their spirits cried out.

And so I sit here with a pen in my hands, arranging the
codes. An insane man merely toying with babbling words?
And perhaps that is all these codes are. If I could throw away
these codes, these thoughts... but they would not leave me
alone, nor have these thoughts been a burden to me. And even

as we, humanity, sought to pursue inherently just causes—tr *pursuit of equality, unity, a greater sense of global peace* *quiet and clean lands—I caught a glimpse of dark times that* *must come to pass. And it seemed strange that to pursue such* *honourable and right and just causes such as these ought to* *reap a better place for humanity, but I could not shake the* *glimpse of a dark shadow to come for a time. But the better* *course will have been chosen to follow a just cause, and* *beyond the dark times to come I caught a glimpse of a great* *Light to follow.*

When, when was the last time that our political lead- *ers were all united for a moment in time? Perhaps at least a* *minority of the Indian peoples and a minority of the non-* *Indian peoples might know that the Great Spirit came visiting* *the House of Commons on Canadian soil on June 11th, 2008.*

Oh Great Spirit, may it be that we might walk with You in Spirit and in Truth...

Sing For Me a Quiet and Clean Land

About the Author

One cold winter day I saw the smoke of the fire drift directly into the north wind. It has happened numerous times during my lifetime, and countless times throughout history, but one cold winter day I happened to merely take notice of it. You see, I had walked my secret trail and sat down to make a fire to embrace its comforting warmth. I then strapped my snowshoes back on to begin the walk back to camp. And as I started walking up the draw into the northerly wind, I was completely engulfed in a smoky world. Yet the strange thing was that the air was beautifully crisp and clean to breathe— there was no coughing or squinting teary eyes. You see, the low January sun was to my back, and as the smoke rose from the fire it created its own lengthening, overtaking, passing shadow which created the illusion that I was engulfed in clouds of smoke. In its own way, of course, it proved that smoke could indeed drift directly into the wind. I suppose life is sometimes like that.

One spring day I saw fresh signs of beavers having chewed the lower bark of certain pine trees again. You see, I had been cruising along the river on my trapline in my home-made boat, the *Dam Hopper*, checking for bear sign, and I noticed that the same pine trees in certain spots were once again freshly chewed. I have never read about beavers chewing the lower bark of pine trees, but I did read about a fellow who was determined to find out what was chewing the bark of certain pine trees in the mountains. He kept watching and discovered it was some of the male sheep that were chewing them, only during the early springtime. He speculated that there was something of nutritional value that the male sheep needed replenishing. With the beavers, I did not know if it was males or females chewing on the lower pine bark, as it is kinda hard to tell the difference unless you flip them over, but it was generally the early springtime when they chewed upon it. Seems to me that life still has a few mysteries left.

One early summer day (it was the end of May but hot), I saw a shower of ash replaced by a shower of snow flurries within an 18-hour period. You see, a forest fire had started some 30 miles to the north of my camp, the flames quickly fanned by strong south winds which switched to strong north winds late in the day. I noticed heavy ash starting to fall like snowflakes, so I climbed the tall tree behind camp to have a look. Sure enough, a large column of smoke from a fair-sized fire was rising upwards and then being blown towards the south. The temperature was quickly dropping, and by morning it was snowing. That is how I came to see a shower of ash and a shower of snow within 18 hours of each other. I suppose life is kinda like that, we never know what we're going to get.

One autumn day I saw some glow-in-the-dark bugs in the water. I've taken notice of these bugs several times over the years during the month of September. I just happened to notice them during this month because I have a habit of lying down on the dock and peering into the dark waters during the time of the wild rice harvest, as the days are getting shorter. It works better on dark, cloudy nights to see them, and it only makes sense that the greater the darkness, the greater the light of the candle is seen. These tiny bugs would glow in a reddish colour, moving very slowly about. When I first saw them I thought I was merely seeing things, which of course all along I was. The only reason I had not noticed them sooner in life is because I had not bothered to peer into the dark waters sooner in life. But I suppose that life is kinda like that sometimes.

To breathe in is to know I am alive, and to breathe out is to know I have lived. Sing for me a quiet and clean land that breathes well.

Sing For Me a Quiet and Clean La